Unless otherwise noted, all Scripture quotations are from the *New King James Version.* Copyright © 1979, 1980, 1982 by Thomas Nelson, Inc., Nashville, Tennessee.

ISBN 0-9651421-0-8
Printed in the United States of America

Come Home America

Daniel E. Johnson

For Martha

WHO RODE
WITH ME
ON THE
𝔑𝔦𝔤𝔥𝔱 𝔗𝔯𝔞𝔦𝔫 𝔱𝔬 𝔐𝔢𝔪𝔭𝔥𝔦𝔰

CONTENTS

1

Whatever Happened to America?

The time for excuses is over, the returns are in on the Brave New World of liberal social policy, and they are not good. We now know that the left was peddling from an empty wagon. . . .
— William J. Bennett

And while men slept, the enemy sowed tares.
— the Bible

As a midwesterner now living in the Pacific Northwest, I was both fascinated and curious when I first visited New England a few years ago. The harbors, hills, and rolling countryside with its quaint villages and bustling cities evoked memories of life as it might have been 200 years ago.

Again and again I returned to the cradle of American liberty. As I crisscrossed the New World of our ancestors, I sought out the old churches, studied the landmarks, visited historic sights, drove the back roads, and searched the libraries. All the while, a question haunted me — Whatever happened to the America our forefathers established?

What went wrong? Where did we turn aside?

New England's great colleges and universities, initially established for the training of young ministers, are now bastions of theological liberalism and social activism.

I thought of the revival at Yale University in 1795, when its president, Timothy Dwight, challenged the atheism and immorality of its students.

I remembered John Harvard, who donated his library and half of his estate to found a university whose official motto was "For Christ and the Church," and I wondered at the ignorance of history and betrayal of trust reflected in Jane Fonda's recent visit to Harvard University where she spoke of "the myth of Christianity."

Then I thought of Jonathan Edwards; David Brainerd and Adonirum Judson; the Tennents, father and sons; the Wesleys and George Whitefield — stellar figures who left a lasting impression on our young nation.

In light of the direction our nation is heading today, I must ask: At what point did we choose the wrong road? Was it a sudden or gradual descent? Did we leap, or were we pushed? Were we deceived, or did we deliberately do ourselves in?

Fascinated, and at the same time troubled, by these questions, I set out to find some answers.

Impelling Curiosity or Divine Mandate?

I stood at Plymouth Rock one chilly autumn afternoon and imagined a similar day in 1620, when the small group of Pilgrims landed here. Who were these strangers, I wondered, who abandoned hearth and home for the wilderness of a new world? Why did they brave the stormy North Atlantic?

I knew the facts about the early voyagers and adventurers, but the motivation behind their coming to America had never been clear to me. Thinking a book on the history of the United States — a text widely used in our public schools — would shed some light on my search, I picked it up and began to read.

"Impelling curiosity," the author of this text wrote, "was one of the prime forces that drove adventuresome Europeans to sail westward across the uncharted Atlantic to come by surprise upon a great wilderness later called America."

I put the book down and exclaimed, "Impelling curiosity!"

Tell that to William Bradford and George Carver, who, in the words of Peter Marshall, sat "beneath the swinging lantern in the cabin of the *Mayflower* affixing their signatures to the solemn declaration establishing the Commonwealth of Massachusetts," knowing full well they were risking their lives by doing so.

Why did they do it? For the sake of impelling curiosity? Half of those who came on the *Mayflower* died that first winter.

Instead of relying on secular texts, I decided to search out books written by Christian scholars on the founding of our nation. From the early writings of our forefathers, I became convinced that the *Mayflower* Pilgrims came for political, religious, and economic liberty — and to bring the gospel of Jesus Christ to these shores — as had the earlier settlers who had landed in 1607 and formed the Jamestown colony.

It wasn't impelling curiosity that drove our ancestors to leave the relative safety of their homes in Europe and sail an uncharted sea to come to an unknown land. They came for political, economic, and religious freedom.

Many Americans are ignorant of these facts. Why? Because America's history has been rewritten in the past 50 years to camouflage our forefathers' Christian commitment.

Formerly members of the Church of England, the Puritans believed in the inerrant Word of God and sought to worship God without all the rituals and legalism that the state church required. The Pilgrims, or "Separatists," were Puritans who, out of frustration, had left the church to form their own religious group. Believing in One higher than the king, they set sail in 1620, under what they considered to be *a divine mandate.*

More than a hundred years earlier Christopher Columbus, whose first name means "Christ bearer," had also sailed west with the intention of bringing the gospel to the pagans. Those who try to rewrite history would have us believe otherwise, but Columbus' own writings prove that his intentions were honorable. Whatever faults he may have had and whatever misconduct might be ascribed to him in later life, he considered his mission to be ordained and directed by God.

The early settlers, for whom Columbus had charted the way, came to establish a beachhead from which the gospel of Jesus Christ could be taken to the ends of the earth. They came because they knew God and wanted something better for their children than the old country could offer.

The great patriot Patrick Henry made this point when he said:

> It cannot be emphasized too strongly or too often that this great nation was founded not by religionists, but by Christians; not by religion, but by the gospel of Jesus Christ.

One secular encyclopedia notes that the Puritans

came to "dominate the political and cultural life in New England," then the text follows with this statement: "At that time, church and state were not separated, as they are today."

Why? Because the early founders of our nation came to set up a government based on Christian principles. They never intended for church and state to be separate in their goals or in their foundation.

Who Were the Pilgrims?

While a recent textbook defines the Pilgrims as "people who go on long journeys in large ships," the facts show that the Pilgrims and many other religious people came here in search of religious freedom. Our nation was not founded by atheists, but by men and women who, for the most part, "had an abiding faith in God, the Bible, and His church," writes LaHaye.

As products of the Reformation that swept through northern Europe and England, they had been influenced by the teachings of John Calvin and Martin Luther. These two taught that man is by nature a sinner, but that he can be regenerated and transformed solely by the grace of God and faith in the blood of Jesus Christ.

Teaching the sovereignty of God, the inerrancy of the Bible, and absolute truth, these two reformers realized that personal, spiritual growth depended on making it possible for the common people to read the Scriptures themselves. To do this, however, required two innovative — and radical — social changes: the translation of the Scriptures into the languages of the people and the education of the masses so they could learn to read.

Until that time, only members of the elite, ruling class received an education and the Scriptures were only available to the clergy. Because of their educational superiority, the elite controlled the government, educational institutions, and businesses. The masses, who were farmers, peasants, and later factory workers, were illiterate and unable to participate in the leadership of their government.

What did that mean for the uneducated?

Tim LaHaye explains: "As a result, the undemocratic policies of an elite ruling class prevailed, offering no election, little freedom, and much slavery."

During this same time, the Reformation was taking place in Europe. People were turning back to God, receiving Christ as Saviour, and acknowledging the Bible as the inerrant Word of God. That was the message of the gospel that the Puritans and the Pilgrims brought to America.

As the Reformation awakened the masses to the teachings of Scripture, they began to yearn for a "new world" where they could establish a society based on biblical principles. As a result, our Christian forefathers believed that God was the Creator and sustainer of the universe, and they considered man "a created being responsible to God to obey the truths He revealed for humanity in the Bible," notes LaHaye.

Historian A. James Reichley, in his book, *Religion in American Public Life,* makes this profound statement:

> The single most influential, cultural force that worked in the new nation was the combination of religious beliefs and social attitudes known as Puritanism. At the time of the Revolution at least 75 percent of American citizens had grown up in families espousing some form of Puritanism. Among the remainder more than half had roots in related traditions of European Calvinism.

What were these "social attitudes" of Puritanism that

had such an impact on the thinking of America's first government leaders? Reichley explains:

> The great idea of Puritanism, as of the entire Reformation, was the total sovereignty and awesome otherness of God. Separated from all things human, including the institutional church, by a vast spiritual and moral gulf crossable only by the infinitude of God's grace and love. . . . Mainline Puritanism regarded human society as tainted by sin but, nevertheless, potentially useful to religion.
>
> The biblical model of "a city on a hill" was the relevant goal for political action. Puritan divines called for establishment of a "Holy Community," governed according to standards derived from Christian principals of morality and justice.

The establishment of this "Holy Community" centered around the church. The Congregational Church, officially established in three of the four New England colonies, had its roots in Puritanism. The Puritans' influence was also found in the South and the middle Colonies, where the Anglican Church had become predominant.

Although it is unlikely that all these early settlers were born-again Christians, they, with rare exception, recognized the value of the Bible and the importance of faith in God.

In his book, *One Nation Under God,* James C. Hefley notes that the Pilgrims' famous Mayflower Compact, which is omitted from many school textbooks today, said in part,

> We are knit together in a body in a strict and

sacred bond and covenant of the Lord of the violation whereof we make great conscience and by virtue whereof we do hold ourselves strictly tied to all care of each other's good and of the whole by everyone and so mutually.

Mel and Norma Gabler, writing in their book, *What Are They Teaching Our Children?* mention "the fundamental orders of Connecticut," in which Pastor Thomas Hooker called for an "orderly and decent government according to God." This important document became the first state constitution and was later the prototype for the Constitution of the United States.

William Penn, a devout Quaker, stated his desire to establish Pennsylvania as a "holy experiment" in religious and political freedom. What a rich and wonderful heritage we, as Christians, share with our forefathers!

Thwarting that Old Deluder

The community church, however, became more than a place of worship. It was also the center of education. Since the minister of the church was usually an educated man — and may have been the only person who owned a Bible — he also became the teacher.

The primary purpose of education was to enable the people to pursue the truth for themselves. Puritan parents wanted their children to read the inspired Scriptures and hear from God directly instead of second hand. For that reason, the Bible was considered the most important part of the curriculum in the many church-sponsored schools.

The first colonial school, established in 1607 at the Jamestown colony in Virginia, was taught by the Rev. Patrick Copeland, captain of a British ship that brought colonists to the New World. His goal was to teach children "religion, stability of life, and human living."

In 1633, Dutch Protestants established the first school in New Netherlands, which was later named New York.

In New England, a school system was set up in 1647, requiring each community with 50 or more families to hire a school master. Church-related community schools, all teaching the Bible, soon sprang up in other colonies. The purpose of these schools, according to a 1647 law passed by the Massachusetts Bay colony for the education of children, was to thwart "that old deluder, Satan" whose aim is "to keep man from knowledge of the Scriptures."

The New England Primer, the colonies' major textbook for the first 150 years, contained wise sayings and Bible verses. Children learned the letters of the alphabet by associating each letter with a Bible verse.

The letter "A," was followed by: "A wise son makes a glad father, but a foolish son is the heaviness of his mother." After the letter "B," students repeated, "Better is a little with the fear of the Lord, than great treasure and trouble therewith." With the letter "C," children learned: "Come unto me all ye who labor and are heavy laden, and I will give you rest."

Students also learned to pronounce words by studying the words in the Bible.

In the catechism section of the *Primer,* the first question is: "What is the chief end of man?" Answer: "Man's chief end is to know God and fully to enjoy Him forever."

In addition, the Ten Commandments were taught, and students were expected to answer questions about each commandment.

Such were the lessons learned by James Madison, George Washington, Patrick Henry, Thomas Jefferson, Benjamin Franklin, and every other school student for 200 years — until the early twentieth century.

America's Educational Heritage

Education was of primary importance to the early Americans.

In 1636, only 16 years after the Pilgrims landed at Plymouth Rock, Reverend John Harvard contributed his library and property for the founding of the first college in the colonies. Originally instituted "to train illiterate clergy," Harvard, along with Yale and Princeton, also became the major training source for America's first school teachers. As a result of their biblical education, these teachers incorporated Christian morals and values in the teaching of the young.

During the next 100 years, these godly educators would leave a profound influence on the generation that would eventually lead a revolution against the British and establish the most democratic nation in the history of the world.

Ralph Reed, executive director of the Christian Coalition, writing in *The Wall Street Journal,* sums up America's educational heritage:

> Unique among all nations in history, America was settled by people of faith. Our educational system was largely founded by clergy. Jonathan Edwards, one of the first presidents of Princeton, stirred congregations with sermons that warned of "sinners in the hands of an angry God." School children in early America read McGuffey readers by candlelight, memorizing Scripture verses and church hymns.

Few people realize that Noah Webster was a deeply committed Christian who served nine terms in the Connecticut legislature, three terms in the Massachusetts legislature, and four terms as a federal judge. He also founded a college, mastered 28 languages, and wrote the first spellers and primers in the 1780s.

When, in 1828, Webster published the first American dictionary, which was a 26-year project, he used Christian definitions for every word in the English language and Scripture verses at the end of every definition. For over a hundred years, every school child learned to use the dictionary by soaking in the truths of the Christian faith that were contained in Webster's dictionary.

Rev. Peter Marshall, in his sermon series, "Education In America: The Biblical Basis," includes some fascinating facts about the great educator, Noah Webster, who wrote books on science, history, and government. This was his philosophy of education: "The education of youth is an employment of more consequence than making laws and preaching the gospel because it lays the foundation on which both law and gospel rest for success."

In the preface to his *History of the United States,* Webster writes,

> The brief exposition of the Constitution of the United States will unfold to young persons the principles of republican government. It is the sincere desire of the writer that our citizens should early understand that the genuine source of correct republican principles is the Bible, particularly the New Testament, or the Christian religion.

Ralph Reed, in writing of Noah Webster notes, "There was no false dichotomy between personal faith and public service in his day."

That statement could apply to almost all of our American forefathers.

Carrying the World's Hopes

The commitment of these early settlers to establish a "covenant" nation permeated every aspect of early American life. We can read it today in their documents, their laws, their business transactions, their textbooks, their family life, and in their preaching.

From 1738 to 1760, the colonies experienced the Great Awakening during which God raised up men like Nathaniel Appleton; Jonathan Edwards of North Hampton, Massachusetts; and William Tennent and his sons. English evangelists George Whitefield and the Wesley brothers also came to the colonies to preach the message of salvation, turning many people back to God.

In *Return of the Puritans,* author Patricia O. Brooks writes about Nathaniel Appleton, the pastor of the First Church of Cambridge. While preaching on May 26, 1742, to an audience that included the governor of the Massachusetts Bay Colony, this great Christian statesman presented a bold challenge:

> Do we wonder that in the beginning to construct our nation in accordance with this Mayflower Compact, the first building of note the Pilgrim fathers constructed was a Christian church? There was no other way of beginning for them, and there is no other way of continuing for us. . . . That is the way Plymouth Rock was taken possession of.
>
> Take Plymouth Rock out of the Republic, and the Republic will fall to pieces in the very first storms upon the sands of infidelity. As Christian patriots, there is only one cry in our souls and this is, "America for Christ — Christ for America."

Let every instinct of our being say, "Let
that nation be saved and be saved at once
that carries the world's largest hopes and
the world's final destinies."

It was under this kind of preaching that the future
statesmen of our young nation learned their patriotic and
Christian duty — which, to them, was inseparable.

Many historians believe the Great Awakening provided the colonists with "the mental and moral toughness
to declare their independence from England and endure
the rigors of the Revolutionary War," which lasted for
seven years (1775-1781). In fact, the final defeat of the
well-trained British army was attributed by many to "the
strong hand of providence," writes Tim LaHaye.

"God Governs in the Affairs of Men"

As I contemplate that dramatic time, scenes from our
nation's Revolution reappear, and, like the words of this
anonymous prose, a thousand memories flash across my
mind:

Washington unsheathing his sword under a
Cambridge elm;
The bloody slopes of Bunker Hill;
The death of Montgomery under the
walls of Quebec;
Nathan Hale saying, "I only regret that
I have but one life to lose for my country;"
The prison ships in the Hudson;
Benedict Arnold foiled as he tried to
betray his country;
The piercing cold of Valley Forge;
Benjamin Franklin saying, "We must
all hang together or we shall surely all hang
separately;"

Robert Morris, the patriotic financier,
patiently collecting money for the cause;
Alexander Hamilton storming the re-
doubt at Yorktown;
The British fleet sailing out of New
York Bay in its grand evacuation.

Under the trying experiences of the Revolutionary
War, our forefathers' faith was tested — including those
who would later frame, in 1787, the greatest document in
the history of human government — the Constitution of
the United States. These young men who went to Philadelphia had been directly or indirectly impacted by the
gospel preached during the Great Awakening of the 1740s.
They believed in the inerrant word of God and in biblical
principles.

Tim LaHaye, in his book, *Faith of our Founding
Fathers,* notes that "America was built on more religious
freedoms than any nation in the history of the world. Even
secular humanists, if they were honest, would have to
admit to the religious (particularly the Christian) origins
of this nation."

Of the 55 delegates to the Constitutional Convention
all but three were church members. And at that time, being
a church member meant something. According to Professor Garry Wills, in order to be a church member a person
had to confess to "a working of the Spirit" in his life.

Thomas Jefferson, who was in his twenties when he
wrote the Declaration of Independence in 1776, was not
present at the Constitutional Convention in Philadelphia
because he was the ambassador to France at the time. Of
the delegates selected to attend, many were relatively
young men: Alexander Hamilton was only 30, James
Madison was 36, Edmond Randolph was 34, Patterson
was 32, Gouverneur Morris was 35, Oliver Ellsworth was

42, George Washington was 55.

Since the delegates came from all 13 colonies, every member had his own ideas, and the convention became hopelessly deadlocked. The arguing was so intense between delegates from large and small states that James Madison, the chief architect of the Constitution, later said, "Without the natural intervention of Almighty God, we would never have had a Constitution." In fact some have called what happened the "Miracle at Philadelphia."

One morning as temperatures rose and tempers flared, Ben Franklin, at 81 the oldest member of the delegation, stood up and reminded the delegates of God's sovereign protection during the recent Revolutionary War.

Rev. Peter Marshall, in his sermon series, "Education In America: The Biblical Basis," recounts the incident and quotes from Franklin's speech, in which he reminds the delegates of God's help during the war:

> In the beginning of the contest with Britain, when we were sensible with danger, we had daily prayers in this room for divine protection. Our prayers, Sir, were heard, and they were graciously answered. All of us who were engaged in that struggle must have observed frequent instances of a superintending Providence in our favor.

Then Franklin asked the delegates this question: "And have we now forgotten this powerful Friend or do we imagine we no longer need His assistance?"

With determined boldness, the great statesman continued, making this impassioned plea to the president of the Constitutional Convention, George Washington:

> I have lived, Sir, a long time, and the longer I live the more convincing proofs I see of

this truth that God governs in the affairs of men. And if a sparrow cannot fall to the ground without His notice, is it probable that an empire can rise without His aid?

We have been assured, Sir, in the Sacred Writings that except the Lord build the house they labor in vain that build it. I firmly believe this. I also believe that without His concurring aid we shall succeed in this political building, no better than the builders of Babel. We shall be divided by our little partial, local interests, and our projects will be confounded, and we ourselves shall become a reproach and a byword down to future ages. And what is worse, mankind may hereafter from this unfortunate instance despair of establishing government by human wisdom and leave it to chance, war, or conquest.

I, therefore, beg leave, to move that henceforth prayers employing the assistance of Heaven and its blessing on our deliberations be held in this assembly every morning before we proceed with business.

Although Benjamin Franklin was not a church member, he obviously believed in God and knew that without His help, the delegates would surely fail in their mission.

Jonathan Danton, a member of the New Jersey delegation to the Constitutional Convention, explained the group's reaction to Franklin's speech:

The doctor sat down. And never did I behold a countenance at once so dignified and delighted as that of Washington at the close of the address. Nor were the members of the convention generally less affected. The words of the venerable Franklin fell upon our ears with a weight and authority even greater than we may suppose an oracle to have had in the Roman Senate.

Roger Sherman of Connecticut, a magnificent Christian, seconded Franklin's motion for prayer, and Edmond Jennings Randolph of Virginia proposed that a sermon be preached on Independence Day — July 4.

As a result of Franklin's suggestion, the Convention dismissed their activities for the next three days and called in ministers from Philadelphia to preach to them. This was on June 28. For three days our Founding Fathers fasted and prayed, waiting upon God.

When the Convention reconvened on July 2, the spirit of contention that had existed was replaced by a spirit of reconciliation. The deadlock was broken. From then on it was as if the "windows of heaven" opened up, and the words began to flow. As a result, these 55 men went on to write the Constitution of the United States. Every article in it bears the fingerprints of God.

Had Benjamin Franklin not suggested they seek God's wisdom, and if the delegates had not fasted and prayed for three days, who knows if the Constitution of the Unites States would ever have been written? Who can doubt that God has been intimately involved in our history?

Although historians disagree about what Benjamin Franklin believed, his epitaph — which he composed himself — reveals a deep faith in the One who gives eternal life:

The body of B. Franklin, printer
(like the cover of an old book, its contents torn out and
stripped of its lettering and gilding)
lies here, food for worms.
But the work shall not be lost;
for it will (as he believed) appear once more,
in a new and more elegant edition,
revised and corrected by the Author.

Such was the faith of our Founding Fathers.

Come Home, America!

Whatever happened to America? How did we get from godly leaders to greedy politicians? How did we get from colonial Christian education to pagan public schools? How did we get from the Puritans' influence and the Great Awakening to secular humanism and a valueless society?

By what circuitous route did we become a nation adrift, beset by violence in our homes, in our schools, and on our streets? How did we get to the place where we are reeling under the weight of drug addiction, teenage pregnancies, crime, dysfunctional families, private debt, and public debt?

One wonders at the sheer idiocy of attempting to erect anything stable, personally or nationally, without heavy reliance upon God, "in whom we live and move and have our being." One thing is certain: If we don't implore God's aid, this nation will surely fall.

Maybe it's time to dust off the old prophets and listen intently to their solemn warnings. Isaiah lived in a time not unlike ours, when people had forgotten God. Proclaiming God's words concerning the wickedness of Judah, he could very well have been describing America today.

The ox knows its owner and the donkey its

master's crib; but Israel does not know, my
people do not consider. Alas, sinful nation,
a people laden with iniquity, a brood of
evildoers, children who are corrupters!
They have forsaken the Lord, they have
provoked to anger the Holy One of Israel,
they have turned away backward (Isa. 1:3-
4).

And hear God's cry through the prophet Ezekiel:

I sought for a man among them who would
make a wall and stand in the gap before Me
on behalf of the land, that I should not
destroy it, but I found none (Ezek. 22:30).

Jeremiah witnessed the physical destruction of the
city of Jerusalem when Nebuchadnezzar and his armies,
on three different incursions, invaded Judah and took
many of its inhabitants as captives to Babylon. The
prophet was not forced to leave the city and witnessed
firsthand homes being burned to the ground, the women
ravished, the young men murdered, the glorious temple
ransacked and looted.

If you can read Jeremiah without weeping, your heart
has turned to stone:

Is it nothing to you, all you who pass by?
Behold and see if there is any sorrow like
my sorrow which has been brought on me
(Lam. 1:12).

Oh, that my head were waters and my eyes
a fountain of tears that I might weep day
and night for the slain of the daughters of
my people (Jer. 9:1).

What a tragedy it would be for a nation such as ours, which has enjoyed so many blessings, to throw it all away.

Sometimes I wonder why God has blessed us. We are not the most populous nation, only 6 to 8 percent of the world's people live in the United States; nor is America the largest nation on earth. Other countries have far greater natural resources and even more intelligent and industrious people.

What is the secret of America's greatness?

God has blessed us. Why? His own Word provides the answer: "Blessed is the nation whose God is the Lord."

That is His desire — to bless us as He has in the past.

It is time for God's people to recapture our mission in America's cultural war, but as someone has said, "If we cannot weep before God, we are probably not fit to fight before men."

2

Have the Rules Changed?

When war is declared, Truth is the first casualty. — Arthur Ponsoby

In the course of my research, I discovered a book written by W. Cleon Skousen, *The Five Thousand Year Leap.* After years of study, he identified 28 great foundation stones that undergird our Republic.

Although our Founding Fathers disagreed with each other about certain points, they all agreed 100 percent about these 28 basic points.

At the close of the Constitutional Convention in Philadelphia, a woman came to Ben Franklin and asked, "Well, what do we have, Sir?"

He replied, "A republic, m'am, if you can keep it."

What did he mean by that?

The answer is found in one of the 28 basic principles of agreement: *"A free people cannot survive under a republican constitution unless they remain virtuous and morally strong."* In other words, the people must know the difference between right and wrong and be able to choose to do what is right.

Webster defines "virtue" as: "Moral practice or action; moral excellence; moral quality conceived as a good."

Benjamin Franklin wrote: "Only a virtuous people are capable of freedom. As nations become corrupt and vicious, they have more need of masters."

President George Washington in his famous presidential farewell address also makes this point clear:

> Of all the dispositions and habits that lead to political prosperity, religion and morality are indispensable supports. Let us with caution indulge the supposition that morality can be maintained without religion.

In other words, don't even think for a minute that people can be moral without inner spiritual strength.

Modern historian Gordon S. Wood, in his book, *The Creation of the American Republic, 1776-1787,* describes the mindset of our founding fathers:

> In a Republic each man must somehow be persuaded to submerge his personal wants into the greater good of the whole. This willingness of the individual to sacrifice his private interests for the good of the community — such patriotism or "love of country" — such is the eighteenth century term, "public virtue." The eighteenth century mind was thoroughly convinced that a popularly based government "cannot be supported without virtue."

"Public virtue." Now there's a forgotten phrase we need to revive and encourage today.

But how is virtue instilled?

Written on the Heart

During a recent debate between conservatives and liberals at Regent University in Virginia Beach, Virginia, one of the participants noted that the absence of prayer and Bible reading in the public schools has led to a moral crisis among our young.

A more liberal-minded debater heatedly disagreed and said, "When I visited my son's school for open house recently, I noticed there were posters on the walls stressing honesty and integrity. That goes to show it is possible to teach morality without teaching from the Bible."

One of the conservative debaters, however, disagreed and noted simply, "You may be able to write morality on the walls, but you can't write it on the heart."

In other words, only the Spirit-inspired Word of God is "living and powerful, and sharper than a two-edged sword, piercing even to the division of soul and spirit . . . and is a discerner of the thoughts and intents of the heart" (Heb. 4:12). No other book or set of rules has the ability to change our wicked hearts and help us to do what is right in the eyes of a holy God.

It was the understanding of our Founding Fathers that the republican form of government they established could not endure unless the people were moral and virtuous.

A communist form of government or a dictatorship does not need people of virtue in order to function. Why? Because the people have no part in the government. In fact, dictators find it almost impossible to rule "good" people because such citizens refuse to bend their conscience to the evil demands of corrupt authority.

In *The Life of Samuel Adams,* the author includes a letter that Adams, sometimes called the Father of the Revolution, wrote to Richard Henry Lee at the conclusion of the Revolutionary War. In it, Adams emphasizes the need for virtue: "I thank God that I have lived to see my country independent and free. She may long enjoy her independence and freedom, if she will. It depends on her virtue."

What if our nation chooses to despise virtue? Samuel Adams, writing 200 years ago, foresaw the consequences: a violent and immoral people enslaved by their own corrupt behavior.

> If we would most truly enjoy the gift of heaven let us become a virtuous people, then shall we both deserve and enjoy it, while on the other hand if we are universally vicious and debauched in our manners, though the form of our Constitution carries the face of the most exalted freedom, we shall in reality be the most abject slaves.

"Vicious and debauched." You only have to watch the first five minutes of the morning local television news to see viciousness portrayed in blood-red color. The previous night's drive-by shootings and barroom murders are recounted in vivid detail for anyone who has the stomach to take it in so early in the day.

I can't help but wonder if, as Adams said, we are not "in reality" already "the most abject slaves."

A Frenchman Finds the Secret

Alexis de Tocqueville, the noted French political analyst, came to this young country in 1840, and went from place to place searching for the reason behind America's greatness. For months, he visited all the established institutions, talked to people from all walks of life, and asked questions of everyone he met. This is what he observed:

> On my arrival in the United States, the religious aspect of the country was the first thing that struck my attention, and the

longer I stayed there the more I perceived the great political consequences resulting from this new state of things.

This Frenchman discovered that the secret to this country was morality generated by the religious life of the people. In his writings, de Tocqueville described what the early citizens of our nation were taught in school:

> In New England, every citizen receives the elementary notions of human knowledge. He is taught, moreover, the doctrines and the evidences of his religion, the history of his country, and the leading features of its Constitution. In the states of Connecticut and Massachusetts, it is extremely rare to find a man imperfectly acquainted with all these things, and a person wholly ignorant of them is a sort of phenomenon.

Today it's rare to find anyone who has any idea what the Constitution of the United States is, much less be able to articulate what it says! To make matters worse, our schools today do not teach the true history of our country but a "revised" version that censors all references to God and the faith of our Founding Fathers and the documents they wrote.

An astute reporter, de Tocqueville, had tremendous insight into people and their behavior. He noted that the clergy seemed anxious to maintain "separation of church and state," but at the same time, they collectively had an influence on the morals of the people and public life in general. He wrote:

> This led me to examine more attentively than I had hitherto done the station which the American clergy occupied in political

society. I learned with surprise that they
filled no public appointments. I did not see
one of them in the administration, and they
are not even represented in the legislative
assemblies.

De Tocqueville realized that the pastors and preachers of early America had no political aspirations, and yet
their influence was felt in the way they encouraged their
parishioners to obey God's Word and to elect government
officials who did the same.

Religion in America takes no direct part in
the government of society, but it must be
regarded as the first of their political institutions. I do not know whether all Americans have a sincere faith in their religion,
for who can search the human heart? But I
am certain that they hold it to be indispens-
able to the maintenance of republican institutions.

The French analyst found this astounding since in
Europe, church leaders often used the church to gain
political power. As a result, the Christian religion was
disdained by Europeans, and the clergy were seen "as
allies of the government," which at that time in Europe
was often a tyrannical monarchy that controlled and
enslaved the common people.

De Tocqueville could not find the secret behind
America's "genius and power" until he entered America's
churches, where he found the pulpits "aflame with righteousness." He wrote:

I sought for the greatness and genius of
America in her commodious harbors and
her ample rivers, and it was not there. In

her fertile fields and boundless prairies, and it was not there. In her rich mines, and in her vast world commerce, and it was not there. Not until I went to the churches of America and heard her pulpits aflame with righteousness did I understand the secret of her genius and power.

Finally, de Tocqueville concluded: "America is great because America is good. And if America ever ceases to be good, America will cease to be great."

Making a Republic Work

The second of Skousen's principles that make our Republic work is closely allied with the first that requires a virtuous people: *"The most promising method of securing a virtuous and morally stable people is to elect virtuous leaders."*

Samuel Adams set the precedent when he wrote:

Neither the wisest constitution nor the wisest laws will secure the liberty and happiness of a people whose manners are universally corrupt. He, therefore, is the truest friend to the liberty of his country who tries most to promote its virtue and who, so far as his power and influence extend, will not suffer a man to be chosen into any office of power and trust who is not wise and virtuous.

Our Founding Fathers recognized the fact that virtue is crucial to wise leadership. In other words, character *does* matter.

Although most Americans today still expect their elected officials to be moral, honest, and upright, for some reason, voters often overlook — or accept — character flaws like marital infidelity. We are told not to focus on the candidate's "personal life" but to "concentrate on the man" and what he can do for our country. Many Americans fail to realize that a man who will lie to his wife and break his marriage vows will think nothing of lying to his constituents and breaking his campaign promises.

Our first president, George Washington, clearly realized the kind of citizens our nation would need if this experiment in democracy was going to work. That's why he prayed this prayer for the United States of America:

> Almighty God, we make our earnest prayer that Thou wilt keep the United States in Thy Holy protection. And Thou wilt incline the hearts of the citizens to cultivate a spirit of subordination in obedience to government and entertain a brotherly affection and love for one another and for their fellow citizens of the United States at large.
>
> And finally, that Thou wilt most graciously be pleased to dispose us all to do justice, to love mercy, and demean ourselves with that charity, humility, and pacific temper of mind which were the characteristics of the divine Author of our blessed religion. And without a humble imitation of whose example in these things we can never hope to be a happy nation. Grant our supplication we beseech Thee through Jesus Christ our Lord. Amen.

Those are the words of a man familiar with the failings of human nature and at the same time aware of his own need for total dependence upon God.

I heard a minister say that George Washington was a deist — one who believed in God but not in the saving grace of Jesus Christ. Washington's diary, however, in which he wrote his morning and evening prayers, indicates otherwise. His handwritten supplications reveal a man who believed in God, loved the Scriptures, knew Jesus Christ as his personal Saviour, and spent long hours in prayer.

As a school boy, George Washington compiled "17 rules of life," that he determined to follow. Here are a few of those rules:

> 1. Act at all times as if in the presence of God. And make it the great object in all things to please Him.

> 5. Daily read, with deep attention and fervent prayer, a portion of the Word of God, for the purpose of understanding, believing, and obeying it.

> 13. Look habitually to Jesus Christ. Let your whole soul be endued with His spirit and manifested in all your actions.

> 14. Look to the Holy Ghost, as the author of all good in man. Seek habitually His teaching, His illuminating and purifying influences, that He may dwell in you as His temple and take full possession of all of your powers and talents for Him.

> 17. Feel and acknowledge that all the good you have ever received, that you now receive, or ever will receive is of grace through Jesus Christ. Trust in Him for all which you need, both for this life and the life to come. Rely on His merits, imitate His example, and in view of every blessing

give Him and the Father and the Holy
Ghost all the glory.

After taking the oath of office as the first president of
the United States, Washington humbly bowed his head
and said, half audibly, "So help me, God."

Fortunately for our nation, those who came after our
first president were made of similar stuff.

John Adams, our second president, said: "Our Constitution was made only for a moral and religious people.
It is wholly inadequate to be the government of any
other."

President Adams began every day by reading several
chapters in the Bible and suggested to his son, John
Quincy Adams, who became the sixth president, "Before
you do anything in a given day, make sure you have read
at least four or five chapters from the Holy Bible."

That proved to be excellent advice, and John Quincy
Adams became a great Bible student and knew early in
life that "the fear of the Lord is the beginning of wisdom"
(Prov. 9:10). By the age of 14 he had acquired enough
wisdom to be appointed by the Congress as secretary to
the ambassador to the court of Catherine the Great in
Russia.

Later, John Quincy Adams went on to become a
secretary of state, a U.S. representative, a U.S. senator,
and the sixth president of the United States.

In a speech on July 4, 1847, President Adams made
the point that it was no accident that our nation's birthday
and the birthday of Jesus Christ were the two most celebrated holidays in America at the time — both crucial to
God's plan for mankind. The president also noted that "the
Declaration of Independence first organized the social
compact on the foundation of the Redeemer's mission
upon earth," and that it "laid the cornerstone of human

government upon the first precepts of Christianity."

In other words, President John Quincy Adams saw the formation of the United States of America as a way of putting biblical principles to work in government — principles he had obviously learned from his study of the Scriptures.

Proverbs 29:2 says, "When the righteous are in authority, the people rejoice, but when a wicked man rules, the people groan."

When was the last time you rejoiced over the wise and beneficial decisions of a righteous elected official? How often, however, in recent times have we mourned over the foolish and immoral decisions made by an ungodly person in a position of authority?

The Forbidden Commandments

Another of Skousen's 28 principles that became the foundation stones of our republic is this: *"Without religion, the government of a free people cannot be maintained."*

The well-known nineteenth century editor of the *New York Tribune,* Horace Greeley, wrote during the Civil War: "It is impossible to mentally or socially enslave a Bible-reading people. The principles of the Bible are the groundwork of human freedom."

James Madison, our fourth president, considering how far our nation had come and where we were headed, knew that the hope for our country did not lie in the government. This was his prescription for success:

> We have staked the future of our American civilization, not upon the power of government — far from it. We have staked the future of all of our political institutions upon the capacity of each and all of us to

govern ourselves, to sustain ourselves according to the Ten Commandments of God.

For 200 years the Ten Commandments hung in almost every classroom in America. Students recited them, and as a result most children knew it was against God's law to lie, steal, kill, commit adultery, covet, work seven days a week, serve other gods, and worship idols. What makes the Ten Commandments such a deterrent to destructive human behavior?

Ted Koppel, news anchor of ABC-TV's "Nightline," when giving the commencement address at Duke University in 1987, explained the never-changing impact of the Ten Commandments:

> What Moses brought down from Mt. Sinai were not the Ten Suggestions. They are commandments. *Are* not *were*. The sheer brilliance of the Ten Commandments is that they codify in a handful of words acceptable human behavior, not just for then or now, but for all time.
>
> Language evolves. Power shifts from one nation to another. Messages are transmitted with the speed of light. Man erases one frontier after another. And yet we and our behavior and the commandments which govern that behavior remain the same.

The Supreme Court, in 1980, however, considered the Ten Commandments irrelevant to today's society and ruled it impermissible to post them on the classroom walls of our nation's schools.

Why? David Barton, in his book, *To Pray or Not to Pray,* quotes the portion of the ruling from *Stone v. Gramm* that explains the Court's reasoning:

If the posted copies of the Ten Commandments are to have any effect at all it will be
to induce the school children to read, medi-
tate upon, perhaps to venerate and obey the
commandments. This is not a permissible
state objective under the Establishment
Clause.

Now there's a scary thought. Our school children
might be induced to obey the Ten Commandments! At
least that's what the justices of the Supreme Court were
afraid would happen. But they need not have worried.

Many teenagers today live by a completely different
set of rules: "Lie, steal, and cheat to get what you want."
"Do it to others before they do it to you." "The guy with
the most toys wins." "If it feels good, do it."

I recently picked up a national magazine and read:

Consider the scene at a California high
school: It's Friday afternoon, and the students are leaving a class in "social living."

The teacher's parting words are, "Have
a great weekend. Be safe. Buckle up. Just
say, 'No!' . . . and if you can't say 'No,'
then use a condom!"

The teacher explains her philosophy:
"I try to support everyone's value system.
So I say, "If you're a virgin, fine. If you're
sexually active, fine. If you're gay, fine."

Let's face it. Our schools are not teaching values
because many of our nation's teachers either have no
values of their own or, if they do, are afraid to even suggest
them to their students for fear of reprisal.

How will our government endure if our children are
not permitted to be exposed to the only book that teaches

a God-given set of standards — and provides the only means of putting virtue into practice?

In their book, *The Day America Told the Truth,* James Patterson and Peter Kimm make this profound observation:

> It's the wild, wild west all over in America, but it's wilder and woollier this time. *You* are the law in this country. Who says so? *You* do, partner.
>
> In the 1950s, and even in the early 1960s, there was something much closer to a moral consensus in America. It was mirrored in a parade of moralizing family programs: "Ozzie and Harriett," "Father Knows Best," "Donna Reed," "Leave it to Beaver," and even "Bonanza."
>
> There is absolutely no moral consensus at all in the 1990s. Everyone is making up their own personal moral codes and their own ten commandments.

Cable television guru, Ted Turner, thinks that is a great idea. He announced that the U.S. should dispense with "the outmoded and irrelevant" Ten Commandments altogether. "I bet nobody here ever pays much attention to them because they are too old," Turner told a crowd of listeners. "Commandments are out."

Turner then went on to list his own "10 voluntary initiatives," which included helping the downtrodden, loving and respecting planet earth, and limiting families to two children. He may as well have said, "Forget about loving and respecting the precious living child in the womb."

What would Turner suggest if a woman gets pregnant with her third baby? Abortion, of course.

Turner's wife, Jane Fonda, attended the Cairo World Conference on Population Control in an effort to spread her murderous message of "abortion rights" to countries who still value the life of an unborn child over the convenience of the mother.

No wonder Turner and his New Age partner think commandments are out. It's impossible to live by the command, "Thou shalt not kill," and advocate the wholesale slaughter of pre-born babies.

The False Wall

On what grounds did the Supreme Court rule the Ten Commandments illegal in public schools? The Justices said this is not permissible "under the Establishment Clause" included by the original authors of the Constitution.

Did our Founding Fathers intend for the Establishment Clause to be used to make the Ten Commandments and the Bible contraband material? Not according to historical facts.

On the very day that the 55 delegates to the Constitutional Convention completed their work on the Constitution of the United States, in 1787, the Continental Congress passed the Northwest Ordinance. This document was drafted by our Founding Fathers to give guidance to the new territories, like Ohio, Illinois, Indiana, Michigan, etc., which were opening up north and west of the Ohio River.

Why is that significant? Because this ordinance, in Article Three, states that "religion, morality, and civility, being necessary to good government and the happiness of mankind, schools, and the means of education shall forever be encouraged." Note that this government document made it a law for "religion," which the delegates considered Christianity, to be taught in all educational institutions throughout the territories.

Teach religion and morality? What about separation of church and state? Doesn't our Constitution forbid religious instruction? The writers of this ordinance didn't think so, and many of them had helped to frame the Constitution of the United States. It was never their intention to separate Christian teaching and practices from public life in this country.

The actual wording of what is today mislabeled the "Establishment Clause" of the First Amendment in regard to religion actually reads: "Congress shall make no law respecting an establishment of religion, or prohibiting the free exercise thereof."

That statement simply means that our lawmakers cannot set up a national religion. That's why the early American settlers left Holland and England. They did not want a state religion that would impose taxes and set up a monarchy to head the church as England had done.

At the same time, they wanted an amendment that would make it illegal for the state to prohibit people from practicing their religious beliefs. In no way was the First Amendment written to take God out of public life.

According to Peter Marshall, the word "establishment" to the Founding Fathers and to American political and judicial leaders for almost two centuries meant "organizing a government religious denomination." To prevent that from happening, the Founders knew that the federal government and denominational institutions must be separated. "They never intended, however, for religion and the state to have absolutely no connection," says Marshall.

In fact, on the same day Congress adopted the First Amendment to the Constitution, its members also voted to install congressional chaplains and to make official days of thanksgiving and prayer. If Congress had meant to separate this government from the God of the Bible, it surely would not have voted to participate in such obvious religious activities.

The phrase "separation of church and state," which is cited so frequently today, is not part of the Constitution or the First Amendment. You may be surprised to learn that this now oft-repeated phrase cannot be found in any official government document.

In fact, it was only used once — in a letter written by President Thomas Jefferson to a group of Christians who had heard a rumor that a certain denomination was going to become the official state religion of the United States. After the Baptist Association of Danbury, Connecticut wrote to President Jefferson expressing their concern, Jefferson sent this reply on January 1, 1802, assuring them this could never happen:

> I contemplate with solemn reverence that act of the whole American people which declared that their legislature should "make no law respecting an establishment of religion or prohibiting the free exercise thereof," thus building a wall of separation between church and state.

The rumor concerning a national denomination soon died away, and the president's letter was lost and remained in obscurity for 76 years. No one had placed much significance on Jefferson's phrase until it reappeared in the 1878 case of *Reynolds v. United States*. At that point, the Supreme Court justices cited Jefferson's entire letter and used it to *uphold* — not limit — Christian practices in government institutions.

Once again the matter was dropped, until in 1947, the Supreme Court, took the phrase out of context. They did not acknowledge the fact that Jefferson made it clear he was talking solely about the establishment of a national denomination and nothing more when he stated that there is a "wall of separation between church and state." The Court, however, in citing no case precedents, ruled that the Founding Fathers wanted a strict separation of religion from government.

And the myth continues today.

Foiling the Founding Fathers

From that point on the Supreme Court began to use the phrase, "separation of church and state," repeatedly in its decisions. As a result, multitudes of Americans began falsely to believe that the U.S. Constitution separates government from all religious teaching and practices.

This was never the intention of our Founding Fathers, as a report of the House Judiciary Committee in 1854 notes:

> At the time of the adoption of the Constitution and its amendments, the universal sentiment was that Christianity shall be encouraged. . . . There is no substitute for Christianity. . . . That was the religion of the founders of the republic and they expected it to remain the religion of their descendants.

Prior to that, in 1824, in a case involving Stephen Girard, who considered the Scriptures to be a "fable," the Supreme Court, in handing down its decision against Girard, decreed:

> Why may not the Bible and especially the New Testament be read and taught as a divine revelation in the schools and its general precepts expounded and its glorious principles of morality inculcated?

> Where can the purist principles of morality
> be learned so clearly or so perfectly as from
> the New Testament?

In other words, the United States Supreme Court encouraged the study of the Bible and totally rejected the idea of education in America without Christian principles.

Our modern Supreme Court, however, continued to ignore the writings of our early leaders and finally, on June 25, 1962, for the first time in America's history, delivered a ruling that completely separated Christian principles from education. Twelve justices struck down school prayer, explaining that the word "church" in the First Amendment, actually means any "religious activity." That ruling made prayer illegal and unconstitutional in public schools.

What was the offensive and illegal prayer students were praying in their classrooms? It was this simple 22-word prayer that didn't even mention the name of Jesus Christ: "Almighty God, we acknowledge our dependence upon Thee, and we beg Thy blessings upon us, our parents, our teachers and our country."

The 1963 *World Book Encyclopedia Yearbook* said this case, called *Engle v. Vitale*, was the first time in our nation's history that we had separation of church and state in education. In other words, it was a brand-new doctrine.

As David Barton says, "It was not something from the Founding Fathers, and it's not in any founding document." In other words the 1962 Supreme Court rewrote the First Amendment!

The next year, in 1963, two more landmark cases came before the Supreme Court. As a result, Bible reading and religious instruction were removed from public education. This was done on grounds that the school was officially "respecting an establishment of religion."

Few people realize that President Jefferson was also president of the Washington, DC, school board. As part of his plan of education, Jefferson mandated that every school child in the District of Columbia read two primary textbooks: the Bible and *Watts Hymnal*, which contained a collection of hymns along with Christian doctrine.

Jefferson once said, "I've always said and always will say that the perusal of this sacred volume, the Bible, will make us better citizens." Although he rejected all the doctrines of orthodox Christianity, Jefferson believed in the authority of God's Word particularly in matters of government.

Ben Franklin, who attended Yale University, reported that every student was required to maintain a personal prayer life and be ready to lead in public prayer at a moment's notice. Surely he would not object to America's children praying in their classrooms today.

The U. S. Congress, in 1782, went so far as to pass the following resolution: "The Congress of the United States approves and recommends to the people the Holy Bible for the use of schools."

In 1844, the United States Supreme Court made this comment in a case concerning the teaching of morality in schools:

> The purest principles of morality are to be taught. Where are they found? Whoever searches for them must go to the source from which a Christian man derives his faith — the Bible. *Vidal v. Girard's Executors*

Separation of church and state? Let's stop kidding ourselves. Neither Jefferson nor any of the Founding Fathers ever intended for the teaching of Christianity to be banned from public life in America — especially not in schools.

Even Princeton University, which in colonial days was called the College of New Jersey, stated in its rule book: "Cursed is all learning that is contrary to the cross of Christ."

Noah Webster, author of America's first dictionary, provided the real answer when he wrote:

> In my view the Christian religion is one of the first things in which all children under a free government ought to be instructed. No truth is more evident to my mind than that the Christian religion must be the basis of any government intended to secure the rights and privileges of a free people.

That statement sums up the way our forefathers viewed the Bible and its influence on education.

Contraband Material

According to Ralph Reed, executive director of the Christian Coalition, in *The Wall Street Journal:* "Well into the twentieth century, two bodies of literature informed our civic discourse, the classics and the Bible."

Theodore Roosevelt, who graduated from Harvard and often read three books a day, claimed that a thorough knowledge of the Bible is more important than a college education.

In America's classrooms today, however, the Bible is considered contraband material.

In Woodridge, Virginia, a 10-year-old physically handicapped girl was forbidden by school authorities to read her Bible on the school bus on the way to and from school.

In Denver, Colorado, fifth grade teacher Kenneth

Roberts was ordered by the school principal to eliminate from his classroom library, two "offensive" books: *The Story of Jesus* and *The Bible in Pictures*. This Christian teacher was also told to remove from his desk a copy of the Bible, which he read only during recess when the students were not present.

When Mr. Roberts asked why this was forbidden, he was told that if the students saw their teacher reading the Bible, it might influence them to want to read it, too. Mr. Roberts had the courage to object to this obvious violation of his rights and took his case all the way to the Supreme Court, which, unfortunately, upheld the lower court's decision to ban the Bible from the classroom.

Another instance, which was reported in *U.S.A. Today*, February 4, 1993, underscores this trend toward "censorship":

> A Michigan federal judge agreed with atheist student Eric Pensinger, 17, that a portrait of Jesus Christ displayed in a hall for 30 years at Bloomingdale High School violates the first amendment's ban on state advancement of religion. Judge Benjamin Gibson ordered it removed.

School officials objected to the order, noting that the print has historical significance like the one of Martin Luther King Jr. that hangs in the same hall.

What's the difference? The King of kings is not considered politically correct in pagan America.

So where have these rulings, which fly in the face of our Founding Fathers, gotten us today? To understand the impact, let's take a look back.

CBS News reported the seven most prevalent problems in public schools in 1940 were identified by teachers as: talking out of turn, chewing gum, making noise, running in the halls, cutting in line, dress code infractions, and littering.

By 1980, the seven biggest problems in schools were identified as: suicide, assault, robbery, rape, drug abuse, alcohol, and pregnancy.

What happened in only 40 years to make our schools a place where teachers, who at one time had to discipline gum-chewing litterers, now face drug-dealing criminals in their classrooms?

Statistics show a dramatic rise in almost every negative social trend in our society immediately following the years after the 1963 decision to remove prayer and Bible reading from the schools.

David Barton in his excellent video, *Our Christian Heritage,* presents the charts and graphs reflecting America's social decline since 1963. Today America ranks first among the nations of the world in violent crime, divorce, teenage pregnancies, and voluntary abortion. We are also "number one" among the Western nations in illegal drug use and illiteracy.

Aside from being embarrassing, such dubious distinctions are the telltale signs of a nation on the verge of a moral collapse.

The Minority Rules

Many polls indicate that most Americans disagree with the court's removal of prayer and Bible reading from our public schools. The media and liberal politicians, however, continue to foster this false notion of "the separation of church and state" in order to perpetrate their agenda.

Someone has said, "If you repeat a lie often enough, people will begin to believe it." That seems to be the motto of the liberal left and their cohorts in the press.

Tim LaHaye in his book, *Faith of Our Founding*

Fathers, describes our present dilemma when he writes that the secularists — "that 6 percent who don't believe in anyone's God or religion — are maintaining a virtual stranglehold on public education." In addition, "they control most of our television and radio networks and dominate 65 to 75 percent of our government."

It's a case of a small minority setting the agenda for the majority.

Patrick Buchanan in his book, *Right From the Beginning,* eloquently makes the same point:

> America, indeed, is a diverse and pluralistic society, and any judicial decree in the modern era about what textbooks must go in and which prayers must go out will trample upon someone's convictions and beliefs. If tolerance is a necessary virtue in our democratic society, there must be tolerance for the views of the majority.
>
> The village atheist has the right to be heard. He has no right to be heeded. While he has a right not to have his own children indoctrinated in what he believes are false and foolish teachings, he has no right to dictate what other children shall and shall not be taught.

After more than 30 years of value-less education, however, the mood among Americans is changing. Educators, politicians, and parents are beginning to realize that when everyone does "what is right in his own eyes," chaos is the result. Now they are scratching their heads wondering how to teach moral values without using the framework of religion on which to build. They somehow think that by tossing in a few good rules of human behavior, everyone will fall into line, and our problems will be solved.

A reporter phoned Tim LaHaye to ask him the same question posed by officials of the National Education Association, "How can we return to teaching traditional values without violating the First Amendment that separates religion and politics?"

What the reporter really wanted to know, LaHaye writes in *Faith of Our Founding Fathers*, was: "Is it possible to teach the moral values necessary to sustain life in a democracy and still not teach religion?"

"That question must be resolved or there will be no United States in the twenty-first century," writes LaHaye, "at least as we know it today. If moral principles are not disseminated, this nation will revert to the jungle. Admittedly, it will be a modern jungle but uncivilized nonetheless."

How did LaHaye respond to the reporter's question? Here is his answer: "All moral values are rooted in someone's religious teachings. In this country those values were originally and traditionally rooted in the Judeo-Christian religions and that encompasses close to 94 percent of our population, according to the Gallup Poll."

Today it seems the rules have changed. The minority forces its lopsided thinking on the "silent majority" who don't want to make waves. Now the breakers are crashing around us, and, if we don't wake up, we may find ourselves drowning in our own silence.

3

The Turning Point

James Russell Lowell was asked, "How long will the American republic endure?"
"As long as the ideas of the men who founded it continue to dominate," he replied.

I felt I was on to something when I stumbled upon a book by Jesuit-trained professor Garry Wills of Northwestern University called *Under God: Religion and American Politics*. This brilliant examination of the connection between religion and politics in America takes the reader from the Reagan era to the present time.

In a chapter about Democratic presidential candidate Michael Dukakis, Wills writes, "Michael Dukakis, well-educated in other ways, was not prepared to deal with religious ardor."

Why was this liberal politician so out of touch with American thinking? The answer could be that, when asked which book most influenced him, Dukakis regularly mentioned Henry Steele Commager's *The American Mind*, which he read as a high school student after its publication in 1950.

"For Commager," Garry Wills writes, "religion is clearly as irrational as modern art."

Apparently, Commager's secular thinking and his anti-Christian slant had convinced Dukakis that most Americans were as liberal as he was. That proved to be a major mistake for the presidential candidate and the Democratic party in 1988.

The title of Commager's book, however, fascinated me. If I could understand the American mind — if even from a liberal viewpoint — maybe I could determine what had happened to America as a nation. So I purchased *The American Mind.*

In his chapter on religious thought and practice, Commager makes his opinion of Christians quite clear when he wonders how intelligent people can believe in the Bible. In fact, Commager cannot understand how, in our day and time, a person can be a fundamentalist Christian.

As for our Christian heritage and our Founding Fathers, Commager writes that the American people "should have abandoned the religion, which in flagrant contradiction to all experience taught the depravity of man and the corruption of society and subordinated this life to the next, but Americans were not a logical people."

That reminds me of cable television magnate Ted Turner, who has called Christianity "a religion for losers."

A 1993 poll conducted by the Marketing Research Institute, however, disproves Turner's statement. The survey found that 66 percent of those who attend church frequently either have attended or graduated from college. In addition, 14 percent have graduate or advanced degrees. That's three percent higher than the general population. The median income for these "losers" is $40,000 per year, compared to $29,000 for the nation as a whole.

If Ted Turner is the great businessman he is made out to be, then he should be coddling, not alienating, this large group of well-educated, hard-working, middle-class people who have tremendous buying power in our nation.

After much pressure, Ted Turner eventually apologized for his crude remark about Christians. The tendency of the liberal elite to ridicule believers continues, however.

Christian Bashing

Erwin W. Lutzer, in his book, *Why Are We the Enemy?* comments on the recent trend of Christian bashing taking place in the media:

> Christian bashing in movies, sitcoms, and talk shows has become popular and commonplace. So successful has the media been in defining America that most people believe it is the Christians who want to impose their values on society without realizing that the liberals have been doing so for decades. We are now portrayed as villains whose patriotic duty is best served by keeping our opinions to ourselves.

Commager also thinks Christians should keep their opinions to themselves. In his book, *The American Mind,* he explains the "limitations" Christianity imposed on the formation of our new nation by these "illogical" people:

> Indeed, in everything but law, America, at the opening of the twentieth century, was a Christian nation. Some states recognized Christianity as the official, though not the established, religion. Jurors were required to believe in God, teachers to read from the

Bible, and in some states a religious observance of a "Lord's Day" was a legal obligation.

Limitations? Those sound like great ideas to me! In fact, I can remember less then 20 years ago when states had laws forbidding retail stores to be open on Sundays.

Today, however, no one wants laws forbidding them to do anything — except to preach the gospel in public places! Let me give you an example.

When 75 bright-eyed, dedicated teenagers from a Baptist Church in Albuquerque, New Mexico, went to Los Angeles on a mission to witness for Christ and to sing and testify, they were met with resistance at every turn.

The group was invited to the UCLA Children's Medical Center to perform for the young patients, some of whom were dying. When the teenagers began to sing, however, the director of the medical center stopped them and made them leave because they had mentioned the name of Jesus.

In an effort to continue to share their faith, the teens went to Northridge Mall to pass out Christian literature and invite people to church. Although they weren't buttonholing shoppers or forcing their views on anyone, a security guard asked them to leave the premises.

Jess Moody, a Southern Baptist pastor in Los Angeles, has said: "The way America is treating Christians today is the way Hitler treated the Jews in the 1930s." And remember, before holocaust and genocide and physical persecution always come slander, scandal, public ridicule, and abuse.

You don't have to go far to find people who think, because of the image being portrayed by the media, that fundamentalist evangelicals are not only fanatics but dangerous to society.

Liberals always think that Christians are going to spoil their fun or limit their freedoms. History, however, reveals just the opposite.

Lutzer writes about the positive effect of religion on early American life:

> The fact that religion, by and large, has had a positive effect on America cannot be reasonably doubted. Our founding fathers believed that only a nation that trusted in God could survive as a democracy. The ideals of life, liberty, and happiness were perceived as resting on the premise that "all men were created equal and endowed by their Creator with certain inalienable rights." Belief in God was the glue that held society together.

Today, the liberal elite want to keep "religion" in its proper place — inside the church.

Charles Colson, writing in *Christianity Today,* notes that each day brings new examples of secular society trying to purge itself of Christian ideas and symbols:

> Zion, Illinois is forced by court order to purge its city seal of religious symbols. The ACLU, ever vigilant, fights to have a cross taken off the chapel of Arizona State University, and braves the waves to call for the removal of a 17-foot statue of Jesus in an underwater sea park off Florida's coast.

In a small town in western Pennsylvania, the owners of a local pastry shop had always included this phrase in their yellow pages ad in the telephone book: "Closed Sundays: God's service is better than ours."

The phrase had gone unnoticed until recently when

the phone company told the baker that the message must be deleted from the new ad. Why? Because the company's policy allows religious references "only to businesses that are related to religion," like churches, religious schools, bookstores, and cemeteries.

In other words, religious expression should be confined to religious organizations. If you are a Christian business owner, you are expected to keep your beliefs to yourself and not force them on the readers of the yellow pages!

How did Christian America get to this point? To understand where we are today, we must go back to sixteenth century Europe to find where this kind of secular thinking took root.

Life Without God

We have already discussed in this book the impact the Reformation in Europe had on the thinking and beliefs of the colonists who came to America during the seventeenth century. At the same time, however, another new way of thinking was sweeping across Europe and came to be known as the Age of Enlightenment — Satan's secular counterpart to God's spiritual revival.

In his book, *Faith of our Founding Fathers,* Tim LaHaye explains the two dominant world views that existed at the time America was founded: "One was religious, the other secular." Who were those with a religious world view? People who considered themselves Christian. "They believed man was a created being responsible to God to obey the truths He revealed for humanity in the Bible, for Protestants, and in the church for Catholics."

The secularists, on the other hand, included atheists, skeptics, rationalists, and others of the Enlightenment. Theirs was a philosophy that eliminated God from humanity, morals, and education. To secularists, all of life must be considered without God.

Life "without God" — hasn't that been Satan's goal from the very beginning? And doesn't he always cloak his deception in intellectual terms in order to appeal to the mind and not the heart? Such was the struggle that existed in early America — a battle raged to create either a nation "with God" or a nation "without God."

Satan set his sights on the elite segment of society — those who took pride in their station in life and their "superior" thinking. As a result, "this secular form of atheist-based thinking was dominant among intellectuals throughout France and southern Europe," LaHaye notes, and it "exercised an inordinate influence throughout education, literature, the arts, the theater, and other intellectual fields."

While some of these "enlightened" intellectuals considered themselves "deists" who supposedly believed in a "Supreme Being," they still rejected the Bible as God's Word and Jesus Christ as the Son of God.

Such thinking was nothing new. In fact, the apostle Paul, thousands of years earlier had noted this trend among intellectuals: "Although they knew God, they did not glorify Him as God, nor were thankful, but became futile in their thoughts, and their foolish hearts were darkened. Professing to be wise, they became fools" (Rom. 1:21-22).

Unlike the uneducated masses who had to work hard for a living, the elitists had time to read books and newspapers and gather in their private clubs and lodges to discuss the Enlightenment theories. LaHaye notes that such groups were "ideal spawning grounds for skepticism, rationalism, illuminism . . . and eventually socialism and Marxism."

The masses, on the other hand — who as a whole

were more religious — "were not attracted to the secular-istic fads that swept through the minority during the eighteenth century." The common people, as usual, had more common sense.

That reminds me of another observation made by the apostle Paul:

> Not many wise according to the flesh, not many mighty, not many noble, are called. But God has chosen the foolish things of the world to put to shame the wise, and God has chosen the weak things of the world to put to shame the things which are mighty . . . that no flesh should glory in His presence (1 Cor. 1:26-27).

The so-called noble and mighty in Europe continued to flaunt their new-found philosophy, which rejected the teachings of Scripture, and, according to LaHaye, advocated "freedom, liberty, and pleasure." Tenacious in their secularism, they went beyond disbelief in God to open hostility toward anyone who held strong, religious beliefs.

LaHaye describes the tension that existed between secularism and Christianity: "The Christian emphasized that freedom is not absolute but is best experienced as the result of responsibility to God and man. Secularism tended to prefer unfettered freedom."

As a result, this "philosophy of freedom" became rampant in France and "spawned the French Revolution," which, LaHaye writes, reduced the greatest nation in the West at that time "to a fifth rate power."

Where It Always Leads

According to Tim LaHaye, this "revolt against all authority is the logical result of secularism, later to be called secular humanist thinking. That is why secular philosophers are usually so hostile toward God, Christianity, and Scripture."

History professor James Hitchcock has described it in these words: "The anti-religious sentiment of the Enlightenment was not solely a matter of ideas." In other words, they wanted to do more than just philosophize; they wanted to eliminate all religion and the church from society.

Now you know where the ACLU gets its ideas.

Realizing the danger of this kind of thinking, the writers of our own Declaration of Independence decided to form "a new nation, dedicated to the proposition that all men are created equal." In other words, all men should be free to worship God as they please.

Hitchcock explains the reason for the animosity against religion that existed during the Enlightenment: "In all the western societies, education was largely the responsibility of the churches, and the church-established by-laws were highly influential. Thus, the anti-Christian intellectuals also opposed the church as an institution and a social force."

Voltaire, the often-quoted French philosopher of the 1700s, often said about the Catholic Church, "Crush the infamous thing." So much for toleration.

"Voltaire's hatred was not limited to the Catholic church," Tim LaHaye notes, "he also hated the Bible and Protestants." On one occasion, this French skeptic wrote, "Although it took 12 men to establish Christianity, I will show the world that it will take but one man to destroy it."

The Geneva Bible Society, 100 years after Voltaire made that statement, was using the skeptic's former residence to store Bibles for distribution throughout Europe!

Jesus said, "On this rock I will build my church, and

the gates of Hades shall not prevail against it" (Matt. 16:18).

"Voltaire and his Enlightenment disciples may have failed to destroy Christianity," LaHaye reminds us, but their philosophy eventually led to one of the most bloody and violent revolutions in Western history.

Francis Schaeffer, the modern Christian philosopher-prophet, said, "All roads from humanism lead to chaos."

Humanism at Its Worst

It is difficult to realize that at the time of the American Revolution, France was eight times more populous than the United States and was the world leader in art, literature, science, and education. It was also the leader in humanistic, secular thinking.

Many of the goals of the Enlightenment resulted in the French Revolution of 1789, which swept away "all the social institutions to which the intellectuals objected, including the church," according to James Hitchcock.

Tim LaHaye explains that "the French Revolution that was so antagonistic to all religion, particularly Christianity, did not burst on the scene unexpectedly. It was the logical result of more than a century of secularistic thinking."

Although the French elite had believed in reason, "the Revolution seemed to be the triumph of violent passions and hatred," says Hitchcock. He goes on to describe the social chaos brought on by the French Revolution:

> During the so-called Reign of Terror, thousands of Frenchmen were summarily guillotined, most of them were probably innocent of any crime, and few of them had been given even the semblance of a fair

trial. The terror, an orgy of hate and revenge, was strong disproof of the Enlightenment belief that man, left to himself would inevitably behave in a rational and just way. The dark side of human nature asserted itself with a literal vengeance in the mid 1790s.

During the Reign of Terror, the French government decided to cleanse the nation of anything religious, as Hitchcock explains:

> At first, the Revolution seemed willing to tolerate the church if the clergy would promise to be loyal to the regime. Soon the government embarked on a systematic "dechristianizing" campaign. Churches were closed and converted to profane uses like stables for horses. Religious symbols were destroyed. The religious press was outlawed. All religious services were forbidden. Priests and nuns were rounded up in large numbers and sent into exile, imprisoned, or executed. The aim of the government was to wipe out every remaining vestige of Christianity.

This is humanism at its worst, but it is not unusual. Those who try to divorce themselves from God's law as defined by Scripture will, as history has shown us, perpetrate violence and death on those who disagree with them.

As Charles Colson points out: "The heaping ash remains at Auschwitz, the killing fields of Southeast Asia, and the frozen wastes of the gulag, remind us that the city of man is not enough; we must also seek the City of God."

Without God, man always reverts to inhuman tendencies. When will man learn that he needs God, if for no other reason, than to remain human?

Why "One Nation Under God"?

It's hard to believe that secular thinking and its bloody consequences could take place in the same year our America's forefathers were ratifying a new Constitution.

While historians acknowledge the horrible facts about the French Revolution, few will admit that the Reign of Terror in France was the natural result of the humanistic philosophies of the Enlightenment. Why does this obvious concept escape many scholars? Historian James Hitchcock gives the reason:

> Secular humanists have often manipulated public opinion in their favor by charging that religion has a history of bloody persecution while humanism has always been tolerant. When they want to invoke the specter of murderous intolerance, they talk about either the Catholic Inquisition or the "witch burnings" carried out by both Catholics and Protestants. Rarely is there reference to the "Committees of Public Safety," which implemented the Reign of Terror in the name of humanity." Modern secular humanism has been stained with blood from its very birth.

According to Hitchcock, the French Revolution, which "ushered in a period of near anarchy, repudiated the idea that man without religion could make his world one of peace and tolerance." He writes:

> A movement to remake the world in the

name of humanity gives birth to a murderous and destructive fanaticism. Every modern revolution has born the same witness.
It is one of the strongest arguments against
total reliance on man and his good will.

Fortunately, our Founding Fathers recognized the
danger of establishing a nation based on the secular
teachings of the French Enlightenment. They had already
seen a breakdown of civil law in their new nation immediately following the Revolutionary War with the British
and were determined not to repeat the mistakes of the
French.

That is why, when the Founding Fathers gathered in
Philadelphia to write the Constitution of the United States,
they already had, as Tim LaHaye suggests, "ample evidence that unrestrained democracy led to anarchy." Having witnessed the chaos in France, "the religiously minded
leaders and citizens" decided "to choose delegates who
had a deep commitment to the religious roots of the
colonists who established this country." LaHaye writes:

Those who attended the Constitutional
Convention in 1787 in Philadelphia were
selected for their deep commitment to Puritan and Calvinistic doctrine as well as for
other political considerations. Their goal
was not to establish a democracy in which,
"Every man does that which is right in his
own eyes." Instead, they formulated a representative form of government based on
divinely inspired law. The Constitution
they wrote and the government they
founded upon it verified that they never
intended to establish a secular nation. In-

stead, it was and still is, "One nation, under God."

There is no doubt about it — America was established as a Christian nation based on biblical principles.

The Ever-Widening Gap

Although Commager, author of *The American Mind*, considers the Christian influence a negative force in America, he notes that a century earlier the French scholar Alexis de Tocqueville studied "this unofficial establishment and rejoiced in it," when he said:

> There is no country in the whole world in which the Christian religion retains a greater influence over the souls of men than in America, and there can be no greater proof of its utility and of its conformity to human nature than that its influence is most powerfully felt over the most enlightened and free nation on earth.

While this was true of the 1700s and 1800s, Commager points out how little religion influences America today: "In the United States religion exercises but little influence upon the laws and upon the details of public opinion."

Unfortunately, Commager is right. Today, there is a gap between the beliefs of religious people and the laws made by our lawmakers and the rulings handed down by our courts.

Why is this?

Ralph Reed's comments in *The Wall Street Journal*, provide part of the answer:

> When Abraham Lincoln said in the 1850s that "a house divided against itself cannot

stand," he was quoting the book of Matthew. His listeners needed no translation. Shared language and symbolism muted disagreements and sustained national unity even when political disputes threatened to destroy it.

We have lost this common language and with it our sense of common values. As religion has been pushed to the periphery of intellectual life, the media explanation for the continued vitality of religion assumes an apocalyptic flavor.

Charles Colson also notes this tragic loss of common language and ideas, once held by a religious people in America: "In a startlingly brief period, the West has been transformed from a Christian culture in which the majority accepted basic Christian concepts into a post-Christian culture. Its view of reality no longer resonates with the ideas or even the language so familiar to us."

Why are we living in a post-Christian culture? Have all the Christians fled to other countries? Has there been a mass exodus? No. We are all still here. Why, then, do we as Christians exercise "little influence upon the laws and upon the details of public opinion," as Commager has observed? What happened to the powerful and positive influence that Christians once had on American life?

I found the answer to that question when Commager, in the middle of his book, began to explain the four things that changed the face of America during the nineteenth century, and well into the twentieth. As I read these points, it struck me. This is the answer to my question: Whatever happened to America?

Amazingly, all four points involve changes that took

place within the most powerful institution in American life — the church:

> 1. Religion prospered while theology slowly went bankrupt.
> 2. The church itself confessed to a steady secularization.
> 3. No longer did the Protestant church control education.
> 4. Religion became increasingly a social activity rather than a spiritual experience.

In the chapters that follow, we will consider each of these points from a Christian perspective and provide tragic historical proof that Henry Steele Commager — unfortunately — was right.

4

Doesn't Anyone Sin Anymore?

*Things reveal themselves
passing away.* — Yeats

Not long after Plymouth Colony was settled and thriving, the spiritual climate in New England began to change as the close knit community grew and people began to spread out into the undeveloped countryside. The Puritans, whose lives had centered around the church, found their unity weakening and, as Billy Falling describes in his book, *The Political Mission of the Church,* their "unquestioning devotion to God ebbed away ever so slowly":

> Gone were the "first comers" who had suffered and sacrificed in order to survive. They pledged that their children would not suffer as they had. But in not suffering their children were not so fierce in their devotion either to God or man. The covenant life was giving way to change. The ministers preached heartily to counteract the

trend, but their words fell on deaf ears. The momentum was away from that total dependence on God and each other.

God, however, has a way of getting the attention of His church, and so it was with the Christian colonists. Falling described what happened after a general Indian uprising in 1670 took the lives of people all over New England: "Women and children were carried away. Some going mad and others committing suicide in captivity. . . . In their pagan rituals, the Indians delighted in their sadistic cruelty."

There was, however, a positive side to this terrible persecution when God used it to turn the hearts of His people back to Him.

This mingling with the Indian culture had other effects, which Falling describes:

> The Indians who had been evangelized by Roger Williams were eventually entrusted to be scouts for the colonists. They proved that their faith was stronger than were their tribal ties for they were loyal to God and his people. Here New Englanders learned to fight like Indians from behind trees, gorilla style. These lessons would one day confound the British generals who were yet to come to the shores of America.

Had the colonists remained tightly knit within their huddled towns and not been taught gorilla warfare by the Indians, the Revolutionary War may well have been a one-sided lost cause. Before that battle could take place, however, the church would fight a more ominous enemy.

In 1692, "New England rocked under the assault of the occult," writes Falling, as demons manifested themselves in individuals and entire towns. Practicing witches infected entire communities with their evil, and even the church itself was infiltrated with occult activities. Faithful ministers, however, called the colonists to repent and turn back to God, and the church experienced renewal.

Within the next 50 years, the church once again required a spiritual jolt out of their "dead formality." Billy Falling writes about such a time, that is known today as The Great Awakening:

> By 1740, George Whitefield brought his preaching to America. The revival came with him, and God's people were moved from dead formality to personal faith and dependence on God. Year after year he preached to red man and white, never satisfied with his own spiritual life, yet pushing himself through the thirteen colonies to carry the Word of God. In cities all along the eastern seaboard, people joyously accepted God's truth.

What effect did this revival have on the church and our young nation? Falling explains the impact:

> The revival brought about by Whitefield's untiring preaching was the first truly national event in America. God's people were knit together for a common purpose to further God's plan for the new world. For over 30 years Whitefield preached the gospel. He died in 1770, on the eve of the birthing of this nation. By then God had used this fiery preacher to unify the spirit of his people and to mold them into "one nation under God."

The Great Awakening significantly impacted the direction our forefathers would take our new nation.

Who knows? If it had not been for George Whitefield, America may have gone the way of the French and used secular humanism as the foundational philosophy for our country. We can thank God they did not, or our new nation would probably have faced the moral crisis before us today much sooner. In fact, America would not have lasted to the end of her first decade had it not been for the strong "faith of our fathers" who gave us a moral and biblical foundation for liberty.

During the next 100 years, the church somehow lost this unifying spirit, and their once common purpose became fragmented as other issues occupied the church's preaching.

As mentioned in the previous chapter, Henry Steele Commager, in his book *The American Mind*, points out four things that changed the face of America from the days of our Founding Fathers to the twentieth century. The first point he makes is that "religion prospered while theology went bankrupt."

The Prosperous Church

What is theology? Theology is the study of God.

Theologian A.W. Tozer said, "What comes into your mind when you think about God is the most important thing about you."

If theology has gone bankrupt, that must mean our society no longer has a desire to study who God is, His character, what He has done in history, or His plan for mankind.

What does Commager mean when he says that "religion prospered"? This is his explanation: "The church had never been stronger than it was at the opening of the twentieth century, and its strength increased steadily.

Everyone was a Christian, and almost everyone joined some church."

"The trouble when people stop believing in God is not that they believe in nothing," A.K. Chesterton said. "It is that they thereafter believe in anything."

Everyone believes in something or someone, whether it's Buddha, the New Age, Confucius, Communism, good works, religious duty, or the saving grace of Jesus Christ. In early America, however, "religious" meant "Christian."

During the first half of the twentieth century, it was fashionable to attend church and have your name on a membership roll. Without church membership, your business practices were suspect and your character questioned. Even today, most politicians, in their personal profile, will list their membership in one denomination or another. To avoid church or synagogue altogether is tantamount to political suicide.

Commager notes that church membership grew from 42 million in 1916, to 72 million in 1942. Christianity had become such a part of the culture that most people took their church affiliation for granted.

Commager describes the typical Protestant of the twentieth century as one who "inherited his religion as he did his politics, though rather more casually."

Although Commager paints a rather negative picture of church-going Christians, his portrait is probably accurate of those attending the mainline denominational churches where the gospel message has been weakened by liberal "Enlightenment" theology. He writes that the typical church member was one "by accident" and that he "persisted in his affiliation by habit" and "was persuaded that he conferred a benefit upon his rector and his community by participating in church services."

With the increase in church membership came an

increase in wealth. To support their many activities, the churches, according to Commager, "borrowed the techniques of big business, and bishops were often chosen for their administrative talents rather than for their spiritual qualities."

Then comes this tragic statement: "Never before had the church been materially more powerful or spiritually less effective."

As a result, the expanding and prospering American church failed to heed God's warning to a past generation, given through his servant Moses:

> And it shall be, when the Lord your God brings you into the land of which He swore to your fathers . . . to give you large and beautiful cities, which you did not build, houses full of good things, which you did not fill, hewn-out wells dug which you did not dig, vineyards and olive trees which you did not plant — when you have eaten and are full, then beware, lest you forget the Lord. . . . Then you say in your heart, "My power and the might of my hand have gained me this wealth" (Deut. 6:10-12; 8:17).

The American church, like the Israelites of old, forgot the Lord who had brought them to the New World and made them comfortable and prosperous. Christians began to claim responsibility for their own wealth.

I wish I could find facts to dispute Commager's stinging indictment of the twentieth century church in America, but I cannot. Christian leaders, instead of setting the tone for the nation remained silent and comfortable within their stained-glass cathedrals. Commager makes, what to me is an embarrassing observation:

The clergy had been leaders in the great reform movements of the early nineteenth century, but they played only a timid role in the reforms of the nineties and the Roosevelt era. The great moral crisis of two world wars failed to elicit any authoritative religious leadership or even to inspire any spiritual interpretation. And not the clergy but the scientists instructed the American people in the moral consequences of the use of the atomic bomb.

What had happened in the intervening years between the early 1800s and the 1940s? Why did God become less important while religion became more important?

Religion Without God

Liberal theologians, using the methods of German "higher criticism" attacked the authority and authenticity of the Bible. In conjunction with liberal theology, American universities were advocating Darwin's theory of evolution, setting the stage for humanists to seize control of public education. (We'll discuss how this affected public education in a later chapter.)

As a result, it became fashionable to reject the Scriptures as the final authority. Instead of theism, theologians began to teach that man must be his own savior.

Liberal minister, William Ellery Channing, in his famous 1819 "Baltimore Sermon," preached that Christ is "a being distinct from the one God," and thus not in the same status as God. Such blasphemy was completely contrary to the traditional Orthodox view that Christ, as the Son of God, was of the same substance as God and thus fully of equal worship as God the Father.

Channing, who formed the American Unitarian Association in 1825, denounced the traditional view that man is depraved and his salvation depends upon divine help. Instead, he suggested that man has the potential to attain to the knowledge of God's perfect nature. To back up his distorted views, Channing attacked the inerrancy of Scripture, saying that "the Bible is a book written for men in the language of men and that its meaning is to be sought in the same manner as that of other books."

Channing is only one of many liberal theologians who called themselves "Christian" but who denied the traditional teachings of the Bible held by true born-again believers. I can't help but wonder why they even bothered to stay within the institutional church and name the name of Christ without accepting His divine grace and salvation.

The apostle Paul describes these kinds of people in the first chapter of his letter to the Romans: "Although they knew God, they did not glorify Him as God nor were thankful, but became futile in their thoughts and their foolish hearts were darkened. Professing to be wise, they became fools" (Rom. 1:21).

Whenever God is left out of religion, stupidity takes over. When people refuse to acknowledge God's goodness to them, they can no longer think rationally or wisely.

Richard Halverson, in describing man's spiritual condition during the first century after Christ, could very well be depicting America today. After 2,000 years, it seems little has changed since the apostle Paul's day, as Halverson explains in *The Timelessness of Jesus Christ*:

> Both heathenism and Judaism were in the last stages of decay. The Polytheism of the Greeks and Romans had been carried to such an extent as to shock the common sense of mankind, and to lead the more

intelligent among them openly to reject
and ridicule it. This skepticism had already
extended itself to the mass of the people
and become almost universal. . . . all classes
of the people were disposed to confide in
dreams, enchantments, and other miserable substitutes for religion.

The two reigning systems of philosophy, the Stoic and Platonic, were alike
insufficient to satisfy the agitated minds of
men. . . .

Among the Jews generally, the state of
things was hardly much better. They had
indeed the form of true religion, but were in
a great measure destitute of its spirit. The
Pharisees were contented with the form; the
Sadducees were skeptics; the Essenes were
enthusiasts and mystics.

Today, we use different names to describe "other
miserable substitutes for religion" like Satan worship,
voodoo, New Age, Theosophy. The Mormons and Jeho-
vah Witnesses deny the deity of Christ and preach a works
mentality that traps their followers in chains. Even the
mainline denominations confess to a "form of godliness"
but "deny the power thereof."

There is no limit to the "religions" man can devise in
his futile attempts to deny God's claim to his life.

"Sin" — The Dirty Word

Why is mankind so bent on keeping God out of the
picture? Because God makes man accountable for his sin.

Do not be deceived. Neither fornicators,
nor idolaters, nor adulterers, nor homosexuals, nor sodomites, nor thieves, nor

covetous, nor drunkards, nor revelers, nor extortioners will inherit the kingdom of God. And such were some of you. But you were washed, but you were sanctified, but you were justified in the name of the Lord Jesus and by the Spirit of our God (1 Cor. 5:9-11).

In spite of the fact that God has made a way for us to be cleansed of our sin, most people would rather sin than have to answer to God and acknowledge that they are sinners.

You can turn on the TV at almost any time of the day and find thieves, child abusers, adulterers, and perverts being paraded across the stages of various talk shows. Compassionate hosts interview these "victims," providing them a forum for their sinful behavior. But, no one would ever think of calling them "sinners."

Instead, we camouflage sin with new terminology.

The book, *The Rebirth of America*, provides a list of America's new meanings for old words:

God calls it drunkenness; we call it alcoholism, a social disease. God calls it sodomy; we call it homosexuality, gay rights, an alternate lifestyle. God calls it perversion; we call it pornography, adult entertainment. God calls it immorality; we call it the new morality. God calls it cheating; we call it abnormal social development.

Recently, when a radio talk show host asked people who had committed adultery to call in and tell about it, not one person responded. The host then changed his request and asked for anyone who had had "an affair" to call in. The lines were jammed with callers who had refused to be identified as "adulterers," but were comfortable with the innocuous, almost glamorous practice of "having an affair."

Adultery sounds too much like sin, and, after all, sin is a dirty word!

But what else can we call it? Author and theologian, Paul Tillich, writes:

> There is a mysterious fact about the great words of our religious tradition that cannot be replaced. All attempts to make substitution — including those I've tried myself — have failed. They have led to shallow and impotent talk. There are no substitutes for words like sin and grace.

"Sin," however, was the first word to be deleted from the liberal theologian's vocabulary, leaving people to deal with their guilt without acknowledging the cause of it.

Christian psychiatrist, Carl Menninger, writes in *Whatever Became of Sin?* about this seldom mentioned word:

> It was a word once in everyone's mind but now rarely ever heard. Does that mean that no sin is involved in all our troubles? Sin with an "i" in the middle?
>
> Is no one any longer guilty of anything? Guilty perhaps of a sin that could be repented, repaired, or atoned for? Is it only that someone may be stupid or sick or criminal — or asleep?
>
> Wrong things are being done, we know. Tares are being sewn in the wheat field at night; but is no one responsible, no one answerable for these acts?

>   Anxiety and depression we all ac-
> knowledge, and even vague guilt feelings,
> but has no one committed any sins?

In many denominational churches, sin went the way of the horse and buggy. It is no longer fashionable among church-going people to acknowledge that they could be "sinners." In fact, the word "sin" has all but disappeared from the American vocabulary.

Carl Menninger asks: "Why? Doesn't anyone sin anymore, doesn't anyone believe in sin?"

An article in *Theology Today* some years ago had this to say about a speech by President Eisenhower:

> None of Eisenhower's subsequent calls to prayer mentioned *sin* again. The word was not compatible with the commander-in-chief's vision of a proud and confident people.
>
> Since 1953, no president has mentioned sin as a national failing, neither Kennedy, Johnson, nor Nixon. To be sure, they have skirted the word. The Republicans refer to the problems of "pride" and "self-righteousness." The Democrats referred to "shortcomings," but none used the grand old sweeping concept of sin.
>
> I cannot imagine a modern president beating his breast on behalf of a nation and praying, "God be merciful to us sinners," though experts agree this is one of the best ways to begin.

Does that mean that we, as a nation, have stopped "sinning"? Of course not. We have only changed our terminology so as not to offend anyone — especially ourselves. God says, "Thou shalt not kill," but Americans give murder a new name — "abortion" — and indifferently kill 1.5 million unborn babies every year.

Menninger explains how this transition in terminology occurred:

> There are no "bad" children only bad parents we were told. A greatly increased emphasis was put on love and tenderness toward the child; words like "bad," "wicked," and "immoral," while still employed, began to sound old-fashioned; "sin" began to be questioned.
>
> Sins had become crimes and now crimes were becoming illnesses. In other words, whereas, the police and judges had taken over from the clergy, the doctors and psychiatrists were now taking over from the police and judges.
>
> Moreover, some of the "sins" which privately gave sensitive minds the greatest concern were increasingly seen as really not sinful nor immoral nor wrong. The general conclusion seemed to be that if behavior is really wrong, it is a crime, unless it is a disease. Non-criminal, non-punishable acts might be unpleasant, inelegant, or in bad taste, but why the damning categorization of sinful?

That explains why the Menendez brothers are considered "victims" instead of murderers for blowing away their parents. Why drug addicts are held less accountable for their crimes if committed "under the influence." Why drunk drivers who use their cars as deadly weapons get only a slap on the wrist from sympathetic judges.

The Vicious Downward Spiral

Maybe Americans are confused because they don't understand the meaning of the word "sin."

After all, what is sin?

Carl Menninger provides this excellent definition: "Sin is transgression of the law of God, disobedience of the divine will, moral failure. Sin is failure to realize in conduct and character the moral ideal, at least as fully as possible under existing circumstances. Failure to do as one ought to ones' fellow man (Webster)."

Menninger then makes this suggestion: "If the word 'sin' is unacceptable to you, I challenge you to suggest a better one."

Some would suggest we label our sins in non-threatening terms like "mistakes," "unethical behavior," "indiscretions," "weaknesses." I must admit that I, too, prefer those words at times when other mortals confront me with my less-than-perfect behavior.

When, however, I kneel in prayer before the God of the universe, no other word will do. My prayer becomes that of the psalmist David, "My sin is ever before me. Against You, You only, have I sinned, and done this evil in Your sight" (Ps. 51:3-4).

When we acknowledge our sin for what it is — sin — and accept God's forgiveness through the blood of His Son Jesus Christ, our theology becomes whole and rich. If we refuse, however, our theology remains, what Commager calls, "bankrupt."

Richard C. Halverson, in his book, *The Timelessness of Jesus Christ: His Relevance in Today's World*, makes this astute comment: "Intellectual and emotional degeneration are inevitable when men refuse God — when they are thankless."

What happens when a church or a nation refuses to glorify God?

It becomes spiritually bankrupt.

Halverson defines it this way: "This is the root of sin — failure or refusal to worship God. This is secularism, the spirit opposed to faith in God."

"Righteousness exalts a nation, but sin is a reproach to any people" (Prov. 14:34).

The apostle Paul confirms what Halverson calls, "the vicious downward spiral, the awful abyss into which humanity inescapably sinks through sin":

> And even as they did not like to retain God in their knowledge, God gave them over to a debased mind to do those things which are not fitting; being filled with all unrighteousness, sexual immorality, wickedness, covetousness, maliciousness; full of envy, murder, strife, deceit, evil-mindedness; they are whisperers, backbiters, haters of God, violent, proud, boasters, inventors of evil things, disobedient to parents, undeserving, untrustworthy, unloving, unforgiving, unmerciful; who knowing the righteous judgment of God, that those who practice such things are worthy of death, not only do the same but approve of those who practice them (Rom. 1:28-32).

Not much has changed since the apostle Paul's time, has it?

Reversing the Trend

Peter Marshall, describing America's falling away from true Christianity, makes this stinging indictment: "As the years passed, the voices grew fainter, until at last they died away, and a new generation of ministers who knew their theology, but for the most part did not know their Lord were content to let her sleep."

One hundred years ago, there was still plenty of sin and sinning going on, but something was different then. Carl Menninger notes the difference: "While the law courts were busy and the prisons filled with perpetrators of crime, the clergy were busy in the confessional and the informal sessions with the problems of sin and sinners."

In other words, people were sinning, but the sin was being dealt with in the church. Why? "The pulpit was powerful, and public moral condemnation was effective," writes Menninger.

Pastors were preaching against sin, calling it for what it is and offering no excuses for any sinful behavior. Why? Because they knew, as Carl Menninger writes: "It does little good to repent a symptom, but it does great harm *not* to repent a sin."

Only when sin is repented of and dealt with by the blood of Jesus Christ can a person find forgiveness and freedom from guilt. Pastors who know this and live this way themselves can have tremendous impact on their congregations, their communities, and their nation.

Sounding more like a prophet than a psychiatrist, Dr. Menninger confirms the power of biblical preaching:

> The minister standing before his flock week after week speaking to them for half an hour under ascetic and hallowed auspices has an unparalleled opportunity to lighten burdens, interrupt and redirect circular thinking, relieve the pressure of guilt feelings and their self-punishment, and inspire individual and social improvement.
>
> Clergymen have a golden opportunity to prevent some of the accumulated appre-

hensions, guilt, aggressive action, and other roots of later mental suffering and mental disease.

How? Preach! Tell it like it is, say it from the pulpit, cry it from the housetops! What shall we cry?

Cry comfort, cry repentance, cry hope because recognition of our part in the world transgression is the only remaining hope.

If we don't preach against sin, who will? If Christians pastors and church leaders do not raise a voice of protest against the downward moral spiral taking place in our nation, who will?

You can be sure the media won't. And we can't depend on politicians, be they Democrats or Republicans or Independents.

The call to repentance must come from God's people. If we, as Christians, don't call America to turn from her sin, no one else will.

Instead of a bankrupt theology, we need a theology, as Halverson suggests, that recognizes God for who He is: "High and lifted up, omnipotent, omnipresent, omniscient, one God in three persons, Father, Son, and Holy Spirit."

We must acknowledge our Saviour, Jesus Christ, the eternally begotten Son of God, and our doctrine must include "the virgin birth, the sinless life, and the authoritative and gracious ministry, the vicarious death, the literal resurrection, and the ascension to the Father, and His promise to come again."

If the Church will simply preach the gospel, it will regain its rightful place in our society as a powerful force for good and godliness, thus assuring a secure future for our people.

5

A Christ without a Cross

If gold ruste, what shall iren doo?
Chaucer

*For since, in the wisdom of God, the
world through wisdom did not know
God, it pleased God through the
foolishness of the message preached to
save those who believe.* — The Bible

What does secular mean? An older version of Webster's Dictionary defines it this way: "Of or pertaining to the worldly or temporal as distinguished from the spiritual or eternal."

Richard Halverson defines secularism as "the spirit opposed to faith in God." In other words, anything secular has the world's stamp of approval on it.

The second of the four points that Commager says changed America also took place within the most powerful institution in American life — the church. He says that during the nineteenth and twentieth centuries "the church itself confessed to a steady secularization." In other words, the church became worldly.

If the church became steadily more secular, then it

was seeking the world's approval instead of God's. As a result, the church lost its power and influence over society, leaving America without spiritual leadership.

How did this happen? As we discussed in an earlier chapter, the influence of Europe's Age of Enlightenment overtook the educational institutions of America in the eighteenth and nineteenth centuries, causing many to turn from faith in God to faith in man.

Tim LaHaye notes that when this country was founded, "both the citizens at large and their principle institutions — government, education, media, and church — were controlled largely by those who believed in God, or had a basic respect for the Christian faith." While most Americans still hold to those religious beliefs, the government, the media, and education today are overwhelmingly controlled by secularists.

As a result, LaHaye writes, "A minority of secularists control the lives of a predominantly religious people."

How did that happen? Why did religious Americans lose control of their culture's most vital institutions?

One reason suggested by Tim LaHaye was the way Christians viewed their purpose in society during the first two decades of this century.

With the rising tide of secularism and humanism infecting the country's higher institutions of learning, the fundamentalists started Bible schools, Christian colleges, and seminaries. The positive impact that educational institutions like Wheaton College, Moody Bible Institute, Houghton College, and others have had on the church is unquestioned. By producing many great Christian leaders, Christian educators, and others who have been influential in the "born-again" movement, they have helped keep Bible-believing Christianity on track.

On the other hand, Tim LaHaye notes that some of these schools, "which were largely influenced by the

Pietistic movement didn't train young people for the fields of law, government, media, and secular education. In fact, some even discouraged Christians from participating in these very important fields."

For over 100 years, from 1850 to 1950, certain occupations were considered "worldly" and not the highest "calling" for Christians.

What were the consequences? "With the development of technology and television," LaHaye writes, "such fields have been filled by secularists in numbers far out of proportion to the religious beliefs and yearnings of the American people."

Our Founding Fathers, however, encouraged Christians who could afford it to serve their community through responsible civic activities.

The Sinking Secular Society

When a society becomes secular, the results can be devastating, as columnist Mona Charen writes:

> All major institutions of American society — the family, churches, synagogues, universities, schools, and government — have lost their moral bearings. Simple distinctions between right and wrong once taught and enforced by those institutions have been swamped by trendy notions with often disastrous results.

Why does this happen?

Charles Colson, writing in the *Imprimis* newsletter published by Hillsdale College, explains as he speaks to Americans living in an ever-increasing secular society today:

> A secular state cannot cultivate virtue —

an old-fashioned word you don't hear much
in public discourse these days. In his clas-
sic novel, *The Brothers Karamazov*, the
nineteenth century Russian novelist
Dostoyevsky asked essentially "Can man
be good without God?"

In every age, the answer has been, No.
Without a restraining influence on their
nature, men will destroy themselves. That
restraining influence might take many ab-
stract forms as it did for the Greeks and the
Romans or it might be the God of the Old
and New Testaments, but it always served
the same purpose. . . .

There has never been a case in history
in which a society has been able to survive
for long without a strong moral code. And
there has never been a time when a moral
code has not been informed by a religious
truth. Recovering our moral code — our
religious truth — is the only way our society can survive. All secular humanist theories, given enough time, will lead us to
chaos.

Tim LaHaye in his book, *Faith of Our Founding
Fathers,* explains that the Enlightenment paved the way
for "three of the most destructive philosophies ever de-
vised by the secularist brain: Evolution, Marxism, and the
humanistic psychology." Authored by such atheists as
Charles Darwin, Karl Marx, and Sigmund Freud, their
views have "produced more human suffering through
government sponsored secularism than all the previous
evils known to man combined."

We have only to look around us to see the results of

a society that rejects God and His influence in their daily lives, as these statistics from *The Rebirth of America,* make clear:

> With the dissolving of absolutes, America's crime rate has spiraled until it now costs taxpayers $2 billion dollars a year. A serious crime is committed every 3.5 seconds, one robbery every 83 seconds, one murder every 27 minutes.
>
> Drug addiction and alcoholism are at pandemic proportions. More than 500,000 heroin addicts live in the United States. Forty-three million Americans have experimented with marijuana.
>
> The United States now has more than 9 million alcoholics. Suicide is the second largest killer of teenagers. Teenage pregnancies, incest, and sexual abuse draw national attention.
>
> Pornographic magazines and books crowd the newsstands. Video cassette stores now market the products of X-rated theaters. One out of two marriages ends in divorce.
>
> Some 1.3 million unmarried couples now live together, according to the United States Census Bureau. The IRS has made abortion clinics, "charitable organizations," therefore, exempt from taxes.

Dr. Francis Schaeffer in his message, "A Christian Manifesto," makes this shocking statement: "We live, not 10 years from now, but today in a humanistic culture. And we are rapidly moving at express train speed into a *totally* humanistic culture."

How did humanism get such a stranglehold on our once predominantly Christian culture? Tim LaHaye explains:

> A humanist controlled Supreme Court, which has consistently voted ever since 1962 to force the secularization of our schools by expelling prayer, the Bible, and anything else religious, has completed the secularization of public education. Unfortunately, with religious teaching went the moral training and character building that had long been a part of our once great educational system. . . .
>
> Now, without the moral training and character building based on the Judeo-Christian religions, we have raised a generation of permissive educators and media people who look on religion as a threat rather than a stabilizing force in society.

In an interview in *Christianity Today*, former Senate Chaplain Richard C. Halverson was asked, "Do you think the mass media in general are playing too large a role in the shaping of our minds and values?"

"There's no question about it," Halverson responded. "Our values are shaped largely by modern advertising, and we receive our truth piecemeal, as in a cafeteria. We aren't constantly processing biblical truth — or any truth for that matter."

Why is that? Because, as Americans, "we want and accept the pre-digested answers that media give," Halverson says. "As a result, we think much more horizontally than perhaps ever before because we don't get the vertical, the divine perspective."

When it comes to poverty, the government has only

a horizontal solution: throw money at it.

As a result, we have had an explosion of the welfare state accompanied by "an equally spectacular rise in all forms of crime: family abandonment, child neglect, widespread adoption of ruinous lifestyles and destructive behavior, and an exponential growth of drug and alcohol abuse," writes Dr. Roger Freemont of the Hoover Institution.

In his book, *Right from the Beginning,* Patrick Buchanan provides this shocking analysis of what happens when humanism is allowed full reign in a society:

> In 1948, one in eight black children were born out of wedlock; in our major cities today it is closer to five in eight. The black family that survived segregation, depression, and war collapsed under the Great Society. The greatest cost of the welfare state is not to be measured in dollars, and it has not been paid by taxpayers. Begun with good intentions, the Great Society ended with the worst of results. While hundreds of billions have been piled upon the national debt, we have created in America's great cities a permanent, sullen, resentful underclass, utterly dependent upon federal charity for food, shelter, and medical care with little hope of escape.

Surely God has a better way of helping the poor, but the "divine perspective" will never come from the secular media or from liberal educators or from Washington bureaucrats. God's way of looking at things can only come from His church — those believers in Jesus Christ who know what God's Word says. It is up to us, then, to carry His perspective over into our society.

You can be certain, if we don't get God's point of view across, the humanists will have an uncontested field on which to punt their lies. And what will be the result?

Charles Colson explains: "Rejecting transcendental truth is tantamount to committing national suicide."

Patrick Buchanan describes "the heart of America's social crisis" when he writes, "The United States is divided not only between left and right. What is considered social progress to secular America is advancing decadence to traditionalist America."

In order to stop the "advancing decadence" and help our nation recover a moral code, the church itself must embrace a higher moral standard.

Losing Our Competitive Edge

Erwin W. Lutzer in his book, *Why Are We the Enemy?* provides some insight into when and why American Christians lost their competitive edge in society.

> Why have we fallen so far so quickly? There are several reasons.
>
> First, after the Scopes evolution trial in 1925, Christian fundamentalism retreated from meaningful involvement in our culture. The fundamentalist-modernist controversies made true believers withdraw, causing a sharp separation between our faith and culture.
>
> This vacuum created a popular moral and spiritual climate where values could freely be rewritten to conform to the irreligious spirit of the age. Christianity was still respected but also largely ignored. Christians formed a subculture that remained hidden to all except those who took the time to seek it out.

What was the result of this retreat from meaningful involvement with America's culture? "The erosion of values from the mainstream of America's social and political life," Lutzer notes. In other words, Christians were so isolated from the rest of society that they were powerless to thwart the moral decline taking place in the nation.

Lutzer makes this observation: "The prevailing doctrine of separation *from* the world cut the church off from meaningful dialogue and influence *with* the world."

James M. Wall, writing in *The Christian Century,* June 17, 1992, explains how Americans have learned to cope in a society in which religion exercises almost no influence:

> To fill the vacuum left by the departure of religion from our public realm, with its diminution of spiritual goals, ideals, and priorities, we have adopted a language that is ethically neutral. That neutrality leads us to elevate secularity to supremacy.
>
> The question that excites us is not, What is good? What is just or is best for the larger community? But, Where's mine?
>
> Having lost a sense of transcendence in our common life, we look for meaning in power, achievement, and success. As a nation we have no basis of measurement by which to judge what is of value.

In a recent editorial, columnist Cal Thomas explains why Christians have had so little effect on their culture:

> America has moved through what theologians have called a post-Christian age into an anti-Christian period in which the old

self-evident truths are no longer self-evident, at least not to a majority of citizens. A
minority of traditional Christians now appeal to the definers of culture and government officials to reflect these values, ideas
and beliefs that the United States either
once accepted or, at least, did not oppose.
But cultural change has passed these Christians by, largely because of their failure to
confront those in control and because they
have lost a moral power from too much
fraternization with the kingdom of this
world.

"Too much fraternization with the kingdom of this
world." In other words, the church has taken on the
secular flavor of its secular society, thus losing its unique
power to positively influence its culture.

Cal Thomas then provides the facts to show this is
true: "Surveys have shown that Christians are divorcing
at the same rate as non-Christians. . . . People who say they
are Christians are getting abortions at a rate as high, or
higher, than those who profess a different faith or no faith
at all."

In his interview with *Christianity Today*, Richard C.
Halverson, was asked: "Why do you think the church
today is so vulnerable to the values of the culture that
surrounds it?"

He replied, "It has always been. Think how vulnerable Israel was to Egypt. The Israelites were set free, but
they kept yearning to return to the life that they had left
behind — despite the fact that it was slavery. They were
constantly being inculturated by the nations around them,
and God was constantly warning them not to go in that
direction. They did anyway. And not just once but over
and over again."

Halverson went on to explain that identifying "with the world and its pleasures and values is just one of the dangers of living in this world."

That's why in Romans 12, the apostle Paul exhorts us: "Present your bodies a living sacrifice and be not conformed to this world." The Phillips Translation says, "Don't let the world around squeeze you into its mold."

Halverson warns: "The world is a constant, seductive danger."

Religious Humanism

What happens when the church instead of shaping the values of its culture begins to accept the secular thinking of society?

Robert L. Brandt, an executive presbyter of the Assemblies of God, explains that the result is "religious humanism."

What is religious humanism? "It is the translation of secular humanism's ideology into religion's terminology," Brandt says. And like secular humanism, it offers, instead of new life in Christ, "a heightened sense of personal life and full satisfaction of the natural man."

When asked if he thought the church today is a healthy exception to the "self-seekers" that surround it? Richard Halverson candidly replied:

> I think the so-called worldliness of even
> conservative evangelicals is far more subtle
> than it was 25 or 50 years ago. We are badly
> infected with secularism, with the materi-
> alism that says, "Live for the now." Gener-
> ally speaking, the people of God today are
> living to get as much as they can out of life
> this side of the grave. . . . Very few long for
> the return of Christ. His return now would

instead constitute an interruption in our
plans. . . . We are living without an eternal
frame of reference and not even realizing
it.

In other words, Christians aren't much different than
non-Christians in the way they view their lives here on
earth. As a result, Christians are unable to meet the
spiritual needs of those around them.

Religious humanism has no answers to man's most
desperate need — salvation. Instead, it relies upon "human reason and psychological processes in place of
dependence upon the Holy Spirit and the Word of God,"
Brandt notes. As a result the Church begets "offspring
devoid of the Spirit."

Religious humanism "acknowledges the Holy Spirit
outwardly but denies him at the heart," creating "a malig-
nancy gnawing at the vitals of the church." Brandt continues:

It poses as a deliverer, a healer, a key to
success and riches, a panacea for human
ills, a light for man's darkness, while all the
while adding to man's problems. It is flesh,
and all it can produce is flesh. The Bible
says only that which is "born of the spirit is
spirit."

How tragic. People come to church seeking the truth
and all they find is deception dressed up in religious
humanism.

Dr. A.W. Tozer wrote that "the Christian church
cannot rise to its true stature in accomplishing the purposes of God when its members operate largely through
the gifts of nature, neglecting the true gifts and graces of
the Spirit of God."

What is the result when Christians operate solely in the flesh? Tozer calls it "religious activity" that "is not the eternal working of the eternal Spirit but the mortal working of man's mortal mind — and that is raw tragedy."

What, then, is the answer?

Brandt provides it: "Only in the church aflame by the Spirit and endowed with the living Word is their hope. Human weapons must be laid aside."

The apostle Paul, facing the same problem in the Corinthian church 2,000 years ago, delivered that same message: "For the weapons of our warfare are not carnal but mighty in God for pulling down strongholds, casting down arguments and every high thing that exalts itself against the knowledge of God" (2 Cor. 10:4-5).

Jesus makes it clear: "It is the Spirit who gives life; the flesh profits nothing. The words that I speak unto you are spirit and they are life" (John 6:63).

Cal Thomas puts forth this challenge to the church:

> If Christians will begin living what they claim to believe — loving their enemies, praying for those who persecute them, becoming a friend to "sinners" (even pro-choicers and hated liberals) — a new kind of power would be unleashed on the land.

Just before the November 1994 elections, Pat Robertson, who founded CBN, Regent University, the American Center for Law and Justice, and the Christian Coalition, was the topic of the ABC news program "Prime Time Live." Sam Donaldson's one-sided "report," which included many false and misleading statements, presented Robertson as a greedy, self-seeking religious fanatic whose only concern is his own financial success. It was obviously a biased attack targeted to build negative opinion against Robertson and the Christian Coalition.

The next day, on his daily TV program "The 700 Club," Robertson explained his motives and financial dealings to his viewers, noting that his lawyers told him he had sufficient grounds to sue ABC for their slanderous report. Then, Robertson said he had decided to follow Jesus' admonition to "Love your enemies, bless those who curse you, do good to those who hate you, and pray for those who spitefully use you and persecute you, that you may be sons of your Father in heaven" (Matt. 5:44-45).

Like the rest of us, Pat Robertson is not perfect. He makes mistakes. But instead of taking his adversary to court, Robertson chose the better way — to forgive as Christ forgave us.

Only when we, as Christians, start acting like "little" Christs in our attitudes and behavior toward unbelievers, will we be able to say to the world, "We have a better way."

Back into the Arena

It is only during the last 10 years that Christians have recognized the importance of getting involved in all spheres of life in order to have a positive impact on our culture. This renewed interest in the professions, politics, and government has not been met with open arms by the world.

Gary Bauer, in his message "What Happened in America?" makes this observation about how the media views Christians returning to the political arena: "Half of our marriages end in divorce, a third of our children are born out of wedlock, crime is running rampant, and to listen to our leaders and many in our media, you would think the biggest threat facing America is that more men and women of faith may go into government."

The "pagan left" as columnist Cal Thomas calls them have begun their attack against what they call the "religious right." But, he says, Christians "can't enter the political arena . . . and then cry foul (or 'bigotry') when they are criticized."

Thomas suggests that if the Church wants to be involved in national politics, it must do two things: get its house in order and "participate on an equal footing in presenting its beliefs and values." In other words, we have to move out into the world — not to become "of it" — but to "slow down the spoilage" by being "salt," as Jesus told us.

"Moral power," says Thomas, "Not political power is the superior force."

That doesn't mean it will be easy, especially in a society that either ignores or puts a negative slant on anything "religious."

Erwin W. Lutzer in his book, *Why Are We the Enemy?* points out why "the re-entry of the church into the cultural debate after decades of silence was most unwelcome" by those in positions of power:

> Secularists had become accustomed to having the playing field largely to themselves. By the time evangelicals awoke from their cultural slumber, America had already become steeped in the values of paganism, the cheapness of human life, the acceptance of immorality, and the propensity to make the deviant the norm in almost all areas of culture. . . . The church is now trying to rescue a culture whose slide has been gathering momentum for years . . . Christians were late in entering the fray, coming at a time when the forces of moral decay were already firmly entrenched.

Today, with the emergence of Christian activists, the liberals, who had become accustomed to imposing their agenda without much opposition, are now incensed "when a voice is raised against their vision for a godless America," writes Lutzer.

And there is no greater outcry than that coming from liberal politicians and their allies in the liberal media. Why is that so when it is obvious that Americans, in general, want a return to conservative values and less government?

The answer is obvious. The "cultural elite," as Lutzer describes them, "are to the left of the American mainstream."

Citing a *Newsweek* article from 1992, Lutzer notes that those who qualify as "cultural elite" are "more liberal, more mobile, less religious, and less connected to conventional standards of morality than most of the public." No wonder they do not consider traditional values worthy of serious debate.

In an editorial in *Christianity Today,* Marshall N. Surratt, a former seminarian who teaches journalism at the University of North Texas, notes that one reason the press is so unbalanced in its reporting on faith and values is the background of many journalists. "One study in the last decade," Surratt explains, "showed that only 8 percent of the people in the news media attend church or synagogue regularly; 86 percent seldom do."

When it comes to the way news stories are viewed, recent social science research shows that the news media have a much different perspective on events than the general public. Surratt provides this example: While people representing a news "audience" described 15 percent of stories in terms of a "moral" frame, the news media used moral frames for only 4 percent of the same stories. By comparison "conflict" was seen in only 6 percent of audience frames but in 29 percent of media frames.

These statistics came into focus for me when I heard from a Christian media source that 63,000 men — mostly fathers and husbands — had gathered in Indianapolis as part of a group called Promise Keepers and made a commitment to live for God and to build Christian families. A week or so later, 35,000 Promise Keepers met in Houston, and 20,000 met in Portland Oregon.

Although I was traveling in various cities around the country at the time, I did not see those events reported in one newspaper or hear them mentioned on any news program. And yet when a church up in Seattle appointed a homosexual couple as pastors of their church, it was printed in *USA Today* and given national coverage!

The bias of the news media has become so obvious that no one even expects to get reliable, uncensored news from the secular press.

A reporter for the *Washington Post,* in writing about the public opposition to the Clinton Administration's proposal to lift the ban on gays in the military blamed the "religious right" and described conservative, evangelical Christians as "largely poor, uneducated, and easy to command."

Nothing could be further from the truth as we explained earlier, noting that Christians are better educated and have higher paying jobs than most Americans.

Ralph Reed, president of the Christian Coalition notes that this explains the media's "preoccupation with religious fanaticism, the overarching desire to use 'wacko's' as prototypes for all those who have religious convictions." Because religion is held in contempt by the media, "a gunman in Pensacola and a lunatic in Waco remain exemplars of religion instead of the pathetic aberrations they are," Reed asserts.

The Balancing Act

I can't help but wonder, as the evangelical community becomes more socially and politically conscious, if emotion-laden issues such as welfare, taxation, economic policy, and nuclear disarmament will divide believers.

"How do you think the church should balance the demands of Christian fellowship with the demands of Christian conscience?" Richard Halverson was asked. His reply provides a unique perspective:

> I struggled with this question for 22 years as a pastor in Washington, DC. I had to ask myself and others, "Do you really want the church to be so identified with a certain issue or cultural position that a person has to hold a particular view to be in church? Or is true Christian community a microcosm of the community at large, where all kinds of positions are held."
>
> Civil rights and Vietnam were very important when I was a pastor. I had to decide whether to divide my congregation over these issues or to insist that our relationship in Christ transcended them.

Halverson resolved the issue with an example from Scripture. One of Jesus' disciples, Simon the Zealot, was committed to overthrowing the Roman empire, but he daily had to be associated with Matthew, the tax collector, who represented Rome's corrupt political system. In spite of their totally opposite points of view, Jesus chose them both. There may have been violent discussions and arguments, but Jesus didn't take one side over the other. He simply lived his life before them. Eventually, both men realized that it was their allegiance to Jesus Christ himself

— not to a cause or a position — that is most important.

"Rightly or wrongly, two people can be equally committed to Jesus Christ and be on opposite sides of issues," Halverson notes.

Erwin W. Lutzer writes about the philosophy of conservative Christian statesman, Francis Schaeffer and his revolutionary ideas about putting our differences aside and working together to change our culture:

> He [Schaeffer] challenged us to have input in the controlling ideas of our times. Our culture, he taught, should be confronted with biblical standards on the arts, abortion, homosexual rights, and the family. He believed that evangelicals could work with non-evangelicals, such as Catholics, in what he termed, co-belligerency, unity for the sake of specifically defined social and moral goals. He also emphasized this could be done while continuing to uphold the primacy of the gospel message.

The pro-life movement has been doing this for years — and with tremendous results. Catholics and fundamentalists are working together, lobbying Washington, and in other ways to stop the insanity of abortion in our nation.

Recapturing the Church

Getting back into the political and cultural arena of our society is crucial to recapturing our culture. But what about recapturing the Church? Could it be that we are so locked into our traditions that we have missed God?

Richard Halverson makes this astute observation:

> God says, in Isaiah 55, that His thoughts are not our thoughts. That "as high as the

> heavens are above the earth" so His ways
> are higher than ours. This means we think
> a hundred and eighty degrees opposite
> from God. And it is very easy for us, as it
> was for Israel, to let tradition become our
> truth rather than the Scripture in which the
> tradition is rooted.
>
> If you go back far enough, the tradi-
> tion is grounded in the Bible. So in a sense
> it is biblical, but it is far enough away from
> the root that it is almost unbiblical or even
> anti-biblical. It is no longer God's thoughts
> or God's way.

Halverson then points out how our traditions have affected the way we try to reach society with the gospel. "Evangelism today has become something we *do*, like a department or a program in the church," he says.

In comparing today's methods with those found in the New Testament, the chaplain states that "evangelism was something that happened when the church was healthy, when its members were in right relationship with each other."

Going back to Acts 2, Halverson finds four things that the Holy Spirit caused Luke to record about the apostolic church:

> The church devoted itself to the Apostles'
> doctrine, to fellowship, to the breaking of
> bread, which I see as worship, and to prayer.
> Their fellowship was just as important as
> the apostolic doctrine because it was the
> *apostolic* fellowship which was the sum of
> their relationships with Jesus Christ, with
> God the Father, with the Holy Spirit, and
> with one another.

As a result of their devotion in these four areas, "the Lord added to the church daily, such as should be saved." Halverson explains why this worked: "Reproduction is normal in a healthy marriage. And reproduction is normal when the bride of Christ is rightly related to the groom."

It wasn't because Paul or any of the other Apostles constantly exhorted the church to do evangelism. In fact, "the Great Commission isn't even mentioned in the Epistles," Halverson notes. Instead, "the burden of the Epistles is the relationship of believers to one another and to Christ."

When we work on these relationships, when we are nurtured in the Apostles' doctrine and fellowship, in worship and in prayer, then evangelism is going to be a normal result.

Columnist Cal Thomas agrees and believes if Christians would start acting like Christians, it would create a power that no one could stop and produce "revival." What would be the end result? "The social conditions Christians now say they want, but cannot achieve by themselves."

Richard Halverson, however, sees no real longing within the church for an "awakening." In past revivals, certain conditions had to be met within the body of believers before God sent revival. Halverson believes that all the conditions have been met except one: "the desire on the part of God's people for an awakening that would issue in righteousness, in selflessness, and in authentic piety."

As Chaplain of the U.S. Senate, Richard Halverson learned two important lessons. One is the importance of praying and interceding for people in public life, a work mandated to the church through the apostle Paul, who wrote:

> Therefore, I exhort first of all that supplications, prayers, intercessions, and giving of thanks be made for all men, for kings and all who are in authority, that we may lead a quiet and peaceable life in all godliness and reverence (1 Tim. 2:1-2).

Second, Halverson tries to maintain what he calls, "the witness of presence." His desire is "for the love of God to be shed abroad in my heart, for me to be everyone's servant, for Christ to display His presence wherever I am — that is the maximum witness, the witness of incarnation."

As Christians, we must learn that lesson and put it into practice if we want to see lives saved and our society turned back from the brink of inevitable disaster.

In his book, *Right From the Beginning,* Patrick J. Buchanan laments the changes in his church, the Catholic Church. One need not agree with the fine points of his theology to admire Buchanan's spirit when he writes:

> Recently at Sunday Mass, I watched as a priest, perhaps a decade younger than I, having improvised on half the prayers at Mass, decided to give the "sign of peace" to half the congregation. As he went on and on, shaking hands, hugging people, smiling up a storm, it was all I could do to contain myself from shouting, "Get back up on that altar!"

As Christians we, too, need to "get back on the altar" — the altar of living sacrifice that says, "I offer myself to be used by God to further His kingdom on this earth and in the world to come.

Let the Church be the Church, salt and light, the body

of Christ on earth, a rebuke to the ungodly, an invitation to the sinner, a comfort to the sorrowing.

As Carl Menninger wrote, "Preach, tell it like it is, say it from the pulpit, cry it from the house tops. What should we cry? Cry comfort, cry repentance, cry hope because recognition of our part in the world transgression is the only remaining hope."

The Church is the only hope for America. May God help us regain our place of spiritual leadership in our society — before it's too late.

6

Enlightened Educators Steal the Show

Nothing more powerfully determines a child's behavior than his internal compass, his beliefs, his sense of right and wrong. — William J. Bennett

The United States was the first country in the history of the world to recognize the necessity of educating all its citizens. Until this experiment in liberty we call America, only the elite received an education. The Founding Fathers believed every child should be able to read and write.

During colonial times, less than 4 percent of the nation's children were illiterate, being primarily home-schooled as a Christian duty, or educated in the many church or charity-funded private schools that flourished — without the support of taxes. Poor children had scholarship money available from sponsors, and Americans kept 98 cents out of every dollar they earned.

It was not unusual for colonial children to have read the entire Bible — both Old and New Testaments — at a very early age. One child completed reading the Bible by age four and passed the entrance exam for Yale University before he was eight years old. His parents, however, wanted him to wait until he was 13, which was the normal age for a boy to begin attending college. In those days, students who applied to any university were tested on their general knowledge in order to be accepted and not judged by how many courses they had taken in high school.

I meet students today who can't read a chapter out of the Bible without faltering and who are unable to write a decent paragraph of English, but they have a high school diploma stating that they met the requirements for graduation. In fact, the National Adult Literacy Survey in 1993 reported that among adults with 12 years of schooling, over 96 percent couldn't read, write, and compute well enough to attend college.

Our forefathers knew something, we don't know today. They literally believed that the fear of the Lord is the beginning of wisdom, and they taught that truth to the children.

What happened to change that philosophy? At what point did our educators decide that wisdom can be had without God?

In a previous chapter, I listed Henry Steele Commager's four factors that altered the course of our history during the 1800s and into the 1900s. In his book, *The American Mind*, Commager's third indicator points out that the Protestant churches no longer controlled education in America. This change set in motion a chain of events that had tragic consequences for the Church and our nation as a whole.

In early America, there was a distinct relationship between the Church, the gospel, the Bible, and education, and that impact carried over into all aspects of life — intellectual, political, and family.

During the first 100 years of the colonial period, 126 colleges had been established — all by a Christian group or church denomination. In 1840, the president of every major university in America was a clergyman or a person trained to work in the church. A hundred years later, however, not one clergyman occupied the president's office of a major university.

A Revival at Yale

During the late 1700s, the character of education in America began to change as more and more young people who had completed college were sent to Europe for advanced degrees. Upon their return, these teachers began to have a negative impact on the colleges and universities where they taught.

By 1795, Yale University's student body was infected by the Enlightenment philosophy, resulting in a plague of atheism and immorality. The chapel services were deserted.

Lyman Beecher, an undergraduate at the time, wrote, "The college was in a most ungodly state. The college church was almost extinct. Most of the students were skeptical and rowdies were plenty."

In an effort to restore Christian principles, the administration appointed Dr. Timothy Dwight, a committed Christian, as president of the school. He immediately fired every faculty member who was teaching a philosophy of the Enlightenment, leaving no room for compromise.

Next, President Dwight invited all the students to chapel and said something like this: "You tell me why you don't accept the Bible, why you believe what you do, and why you live like you do. Take as long as you wish, with the proviso that when you are finished, you'll listen to me."

The students agreed and gave him all their philosophical reasons why God and the Bible didn't fit their lifestyle. When they were finished, Timothy Dwight brilliantly refuted, under the inspiration of the Holy Spirit, all of the students' arguments of rationalism against the gospel one by one.

In a message given at Regent University, Rev. Peter Marshall provided this sample of Dwight's preaching:

> There can be no halting between two opinions. You must meet face to face the bands of disorder, of falsehood and of sin. . . . What part hath he that believeth with an infidel? . . . Will you imbibe their principles? Will you copy their practices? Will you teach your children that death is an eternal sleep, that the end sanctifies the means, that moral obligation is a dream, religion a farce? Will you become the rulers of Sodom and the people of Gomorrah? Will you enthrone the goddess of reason before the tale of Christ? Will you burn your Bibles? Will you crucify anew your Redeemer? Will you deny your God?

Dwight talked about the joy of fulfillment that comes from laboring with Christ and the strength needed to choose the right in light of eternity:

> The most important consideration is yet to be suggested. A consideration infinitely awful and glorious, there may be a hereafter! The course of sin begun here may continue forever. The seed of virtue sown in the present world and raised to a young

and feeble item may be destined to grow immortal.

Dr. H. Humphrey, who later became the president of Amhurst College, was an undergraduate at Yale at the time, and describes the impact of President Dwight's preaching on the students:

> It came with power as had never been witnessed within these walls before. It was in the freshman year of my own class. It was like a mighty, rushing wind. The whole college was shaken. It seemed for a time as if the whole mass of students would press into the kingdom. It put a new faith on the college.

Many students came to salvation during the years of revival at Yale. Benjamin Silliman, who later became a chemistry teacher at Yale, wrote to his mother about the effects of the revival: "Yale College has become a little temple. Prayer and praise seem to be the delight of the greater part of the students while those who are still unfeeling are awed into respectful silence."

The result was one of the great revivals in American history that had far-reaching effects on our nation.

Bernard A. Weisberger, in his book, *They Gather At the River,* describes it this way: "Since Yale was transforming much of the intellectual leadership of New England, not to say the country, this was a fact of transcendent importance in American history."

Dozens of young men were saved and called into the ministry. In the four preceding classes only 13 men had chosen to go into the ministry compared to 69 in four years of revival.

Among others was Lyman Beecher who came to

Jesus during the revival at Yale. His eldest daughter, Harriet Beecher Stowe, later wrote *Uncle Tom's Cabin,* which led to the abolition of slavery. His son, Henry Ward Beecher, carried on the preaching of the gospel, and his family became well-known for their service to the Lord.

"Enlightened" Clergymen

We learned earlier that Harvard University had been dedicated to training leaders to go out into this new country and teach the people so they could read the Bible and know God. At the main entrance to Harvard, visitors can still read John Harvard's original purpose for founding this university. The inscription reads:

> Let the main end of every student's life and
> studies be to know God and Jesus Christ
> which is eternal life. And therefore to lay
> Christ in the bottom as the only foundation
> of all sound knowledge and learning.

Even as late as 1796, the Harvard rule book stated: "If you doubt that the Scriptures are the Word of God, you are subject to immediate dismissal."

Before long, however, the educational elite, who had attended the Sorbonne in Paris and Bonn University in Berlin, "brought back secularism in its many forms — skepticism, German higher criticism, and raw secular humanism," writes Tim LaHaye.

This is exactly what happened to several clergy of the Unitarian Church in America. They brought back enough skepticism and higher criticism from Europe to split that church. Like most secularizers, these "enlightened" clergymen rejected the deity of Jesus Christ, thus alienating other church members who accepted the teachings of the Bible.

This rift in the Unitarian Church spilled over into

the educational institutions. Harvard University, which was and is located in Boston, the same city where the Unitarians had their headquarters, became the focal point of the division during the late eighteenth century. The liberal faction — who held to the concept of a godless, utopian society where government ensures individual equality through laws and taxes to pay for their enforcement — made it their goal to secure the university as their own. Only one group stood in their way. Tim LaHaye explains:

> For over 25 years, such Unitarian secular-
> ists' attempts were thwarted by the reli-
> gious citizens; largely those fundamental-
> ist ministers who had enough courage to
> stand up to the liberal leaders of their day.

Finally, in 1805, Harvard University, which had trained ministers of the gospel for over 169 years, became a citadel of secular humanist teaching. It is also interesting to note that 25 percent of the original signers of the Humanist Manifesto in 1933 were Unitarians — many of them ministers.

The natural outgrowth of secular humanism, which denies the deity of Jesus Christ and rejects the wisdom of God is, of course, atheism. Fifty years after the takeover of Harvard, in 1861, MIT, the Massachusetts Institute of Technology, became the first college chartered by atheists — only 72 years after the founding of America. By the late 1800s, even the Christian colleges and seminaries had been influenced by the teachings of secular professors.

Setting the Stage

Having abandoned the Church, the secular humanists and atheists needed a platform for their new religion. As intellectuals who worshipped the mind of man, it was natural for them to use the medium of public education as their stage.

Atheist Robert Owen founded the "friends of education," a group made up of "atheists, socialists, Freethinkers, Unitarians, Universalists, transcendentalists, and other forerunners of secular humanism." According to Samuel Bloominfeld, in his book, *Is Public Education Necessary?* these intellectuals set out to change the educational system in this country by using the model of European education.

As early as 1830 the "friends of education," established three principles, which have remained the framework for public education to this day:

> 1. Make school attendance compulsory.
> 2. Establish government-sponsored "free" schools.
> 3. Form teacher-training schools that they would control in order to prepare the teacher of the future.

The "friends of education" then succeeded in having the Massachusetts state legislature designate the nation's first office of secretary of the state Board of Education. The group then hired Unitarian Horace Mann as the first secretary in 1837, where he succeeded in secularizing Massachusetts' schools. Mann went on to become the first U.S. Secretary of Education, making it possible for him to implement the three principles of the "friends of education" mentioned above.

Tim LaHaye concludes:

> In short, the educational system was secularized from the top down. Long before the Bible was expelled from the public schools

by the Supreme Court, it had been ex-
cluded from multiple courses by hostile
administrators.

Why were administrators like Mann so hostile to
biblical principles? His personal beliefs provide the answer. Horace Mann was a follower of Germany's new
Hegelian philosophy, which claimed that nothing was
absolute and man's ideas were superior to biblical principles. Sound familiar? That is the premise behind many
public school textbooks and the mindset of most American educators.

Often called the "father of public education," Mann
eventually stole America's educational system out from
under the Christian majority and implemented the secular
humanistic version we have today.

After 230 years of successful community and church-
related schools in America, Horace Mann decided he had
a better way — government-controlled education. Now
150 years later, we are reaping the results of Mann's anti-
Christian, humanistic philosophy of German Hegelianism.

How did he accomplish this? By revamping the
philosophy of education being taught in the "normal
schools," which became state teachers colleges under
John Dewey in the twentieth century. This gave the
secularists a captive audience and the ability to impact the
style and methods of nearly every future public school
teacher in America.

Tim LaHaye explains the results of this "gradual
takeover":

> Today the disciples of John Dewey, who
> was head of Columbia University's Teach-
> ers College, hold most of the key positions
> in these state teachers colleges so they can
> mold the thinking of the nation's school

teachers. . . . It was at Columbia University that John Dewey and his disciples produced "progressive education," which has turned out to be totally secularistic and very poor education.

It seems that secularism and poor education go hand in hand. The National Commission of Excellence in Education, in its publication, *A Nation at Risk,* in 1983, calls this process "educational disarmament":

> If an unfriendly foreign power had attempted to impose on America the mediocre education performance that exists today we might well have viewed it as an act of war. As it stands we have allowed it to happen to ourselves. We have in effect been committing an act of unthinking, unilateral, educational disarmament.

Albert Shanker, president of the American Federation of Teachers, put America's educational crisis into perspective: "Ninety-five percent of the kids who go to college in the United States would not be admitted to college anywhere else in the world."

That statement is shocking in light of the fact that America spends more money per capita on educating its children than any other nation! Yet, our educators continue to turn out graduates who cannot even read their diplomas.

"Change and Adjust"

What's wrong with "progressive education"? To answer that question, we need to know the goals of its founder.

Like Horace Mann, John Dewey was a Hegelian and

a declared atheist who believed that truth is always in process. In other words, as society changes, the morals held by people should change to fit the new environment. That's why Dewey taught his students to adjust socially and ethically to change as it occurs. His motto was: change and adjust; change and adjust.

. Anyone who knows the Bible quickly realizes that such teaching is in total opposition to the Scriptures. God's Word does not change. His principles remain the same — no matter what the culture, the environment, progress, or the intellect of any particular society.

Why were Dewey and his associates so bent on pressing for change in our nation? The answer can be found in his infatuation with Soviet Communism. Dewey, like many humanist intellectuals in the 1930s believed that the Marxist socialist model was "better" for the masses than "American constitutional liberty and private property."

As the first president of the American Humanist Association, Dewey signed the Humanist Manifesto I in 1933, which reads:

> The time has come for widespread recognition of the radical changes in religious beliefs throughout the modern world. The time is past for mere revisions of traditional attitudes. Science and economic change have disrupted the old beliefs. Religions the world over are under the necessity of coming to terms with new conditions created by a vastly increased knowledge and experience. In every field of human activity, the vital movement is now in the direction of a candid and explicit humanism.

Such radical thinking considered "religion" (Christianity) to be a "great danger" and that its "doctrines and methods" have "lost their significance" and "are powerless to solve the problem of human living in the twentieth century."

Thomas Sowell, an economist and senior fellow at the Hoover Institute, comments in *Forbes* magazine that the fears of the liberal left concerning the "religious right" are nothing compared with "the dangers from the enormous apparatus already in place which continues to conduct classroom brainwashing to the detriment of academic education."

Erwin W. Lutzer in his book, *Why Are We the Enemy?* explains that Sowell "believes that techniques of brainwashing developed in totalitarian countries are routinely used in psychological conditioning programs that are imposed on America's school children: emotional shock, desensitization, psychological isolation from sources of support, stripping away defenses, manipulative cross-examination of the individual's underlying moral values."

Manipulating Moral Values

How do teachers accomplish this?

In Pennsylvania, two Christian high school students were pressured by their teacher to read a Studs Turkel book, which included chapters on prostitutes along with blasphemous language. With the support of their parents, the students asked to opt out of reading the book. The school refused and wanted to withhold the students' diplomas and fail them for the course. The school board told the parents, in essence, that they, as educators, knew much better what constituted "proper education" than these Christian parents.

Such instances are not unusual. In fact, any parent who tries to interfere with what the educational elite have determined as "proper education" can expect a battle.

In another Pennsylvania school district, a parent complained that the twelfth grade anthology, *Literature in Society,* contained selections with crude sexual terms for body parts, racial slurs, and themes on homosexuality. When school administrators studied the book for themselves, they, too, were shocked and immediately removed the textbooks from the classroom. The book's publisher agreed to take back the books and refund the district's money. End of story?

No. Guess who was outraged by this action? The teachers union! They said that the district had not followed proper procedures and demanded a committee to review the textbook. The administration disagreed, noting that the teachers who recommended the textbook for classroom use in the first place had not indicated that the contents might be offensive.

Apparently, filthy language and racial slurs do not offend some teachers who feel that they know best what is considered "literature."

In District 24 of New York City's Borough of Queens, Chancellor Joseph Fernandez fought school board members over instituting the so-called *Children of the Rainbow* curriculum. According to LaGard Smith, the purpose of the curriculum was "to indoctrinate children with particular attitudes about, among other things, homosexual conduct."

If the chancellor had been given his way, impressionable young students would have been exposed to illustrated books such as *Daddy's Roommate,* for ages 3 to 8. Smith describes the simple story line:

My Mommy and Daddy got a divorce last

year, now there's somebody new at Daddy's house. Daddy and his roommate, Frank, live together, work together, eat together, sleep together, shave together, and sometimes even fight together. But they always make up. Mother says Daddy and Frank are gay. At first I didn't know what that meant so she explained it to me. Being gay is just one more kind of love, and love is the best kind of happiness. Daddy and his roommate are very happy together, and I'm happy too.

Other books in the series include: *Heather Has Two Mommies* and *Gloria Goes to Gay Pride*.

After massive parent protest, the curriculum was withdrawn, and the chancellor lost his job. You can be certain, however, that won't be the last attempt by the liberal educational elite to impose their "values" on America's school children.

The Worship of Man

Educators like Dewey and the American Humanist Association thought it their "responsibility" to "establish" a new religion, using these kinds of precepts from their own Manifesto:

First: Religious humanists regard the universe as self-existing and not created.

Second: Humanism believes that man is a part of nature and that he has emerged as a result of a continuous process. . . .

Sixth: We are convinced that the time has passed for theism.

Seventh: Religion consists of those actions, purposes and experiences which

are humanly significant. Nothing human is
alien to the religious. The distinction between the sacred and the secular can no
longer be maintained.

There we have in a few brief sentences a "religion"
based on the worship of "man." Man was not created, they
say, he evolved. Belief in God is old-fashioned. Man is to
be worshipped as a god.

Sound familiar? Surely, you remember Lucifer's
words, quoted in the Book of Isaiah: "I will be like the
Most High" (14:14).

Humanism is just another of Satan's attempts to trick
man, as he did Adam and Eve in the Garden.

How do our "progressive" educators plan to oust
Christianity and implement their own "new" religion? In
their book, *What Are They Teaching Our Children?* Mel
and Norma Gabler explain:

> To indoctrinate our children in this "new"
> religion the educational establishment first
> must rid education of sympathy for the
> ethics of the great majority of Americans,
> past and present. They must alienate our
> children from the morals and faith of their
> fathers and mothers.

With the help of the ACLU and the National Education Association, the humanists are accomplishing their
goal of alienating children from the "faith of their fathers
and mothers" in several ways.

Bibles are being taken out of school libraries, and
students are forbidden to bring a Bible to school. Prayer
has been outlawed. All mention of the Pilgrims and the
true reason for their first Thanksgiving have been completely distorted. Christmas celebrations have been re-

placed by "winter festivals," and some school districts have even stopped scheduling spring break around Easter for fear of "advancing religion."

Are these incidents mere coincidence, or the orchestrated objectives of humanist educators whose goal is to control the minds of America's students? These blatant statements from *The Humanist Magazine* provide the answer:

> The battle for humankind's future must be waged and won in the public school classroom by teachers who correctly perceive their role as the proselytizers of a new faith. A religion of humanity that recognizes and respects the spark of what theologians call divinity in every human being.

How are teachers supposed to perpetrate this "new faith"? The *Humanist Magazine* suggests that teachers become "ministers of another sort," utilizing "a classroom instead of a pulpit to convey humanist values." How and when are they to do this? "In whatever subject they teach, regardless of the educational level, pre-school, day care, or large state university."

The classroom is considered the battleground "between the old and new." What is the old? They call it "the rotting corpse of Christianity together with all it's adjacent evils and misery."

What is the "new faith"? "Humanism, resplendent in its promise of a world in which the never-realized Christian ideal, 'Love thy neighbor' will finally be achieved."

How ironic to think the philosophy that has created violence and chaos in our public schools can teach children to love their neighbor. They have had 30 years to do it. Why is it taking so long? Could it be that a "religion" that worships man gives kids the idea that they can do as they please? And why shouldn't they? After all, they are accountable to no one.

Beyond their objective to turn the worship of "man" into America's new religion, progressive educators have an even more dangerous agenda. Mel and Norma Gabler, made this remarkable finding:

> Scores of American "progressive" educators trooped to Russia in the early 1930's and returned with gushing praise for social advances wrought by Marxism. They praised Lenin and Stalin for giving Soviet citizens universal suffrage, civil liberties, the right to employment, to free education, to free medical care and to material security in old age.

Do those phrases sound familiar — universal health care, civil liberties, guaranteed employment? They should; they are the bywords of a government out of control, and it has a name. It is socialism, the very antithesis of freedom.

Putting Parents at Risk

Guess who lobbies for this socialistic agenda? The largest union in the United States — the NEA, the National Education Association. As far back as 1932, the NEA was calling for the changing of student behavior by conditioning them through "behavior modification."

Why? Here's how they explained it: "Conditioning is a process which may be employed by the teacher to build up attitudes in the child and pre-dispose him to the actions by which these attitudes are expressed."

That has been the goal of the NEA since its conception — to mold America's school children into its own image.

This is their agenda in their own words: "Agencies such as the school must assume responsibilities which in the past have rested upon the home and the community." In other words, the school — not the parents or the Church — will tell your kids what to think and believe!

And how do they plan to do that? One way is through "creativity" teaching. Norma and Mel Gabler discovered that the author of one textbook suggests, "If we wanted to truly induce completely creative thinking we should teach children to question the Ten Commandments, patriotism, the two party system, monogamy, and the laws against incest."

In other words, let's tear down all the traditional restrictions on human behavior and make children open and willing to accept anything "we" — the educators — teach them.

Columnist Thomas Sowell, an expert in educational issues, writes about the way government-funded programs are used to control families:

> Much of the enthusiasm for "Head Start" is because it can lead to various "services" being supplied to families. That is, to get the social worker inside the home to tell the benighted how they ought to rear their children and perhaps to give or withhold government goodies according to how well they accept such advice.

Hillary Rodham, writing in a 1973 article for the *Harvard Educational Review,* challenged the idea that parents should "unilaterally" make decisions about the rearing of their children. That idea has been carried over into the agenda of the Children's Defense Fund, an organization, according to Thomas Sowell, mainly concerned with "defending" children against their parents.

The October 1994 issue of the Association of Christian Schools International's *Legal/Legislative Update,* uses this example to show how the United Nations Convention of the Rights of the Child would limit parental control:

> If Christian practices are viewed by a government as "prejudicial to the health of the children," then religious people with sincerely held beliefs can even be at risk of losing their children.

Make no mistake about it: They want your children — one way or the other.

Columnist Cal Thomas gives us a glimpse into the mindset of the liberal elite who are controlling our educational institutions today. He reported in a September 10, 1992, editorial that the District of Columbia public school system, in an effort to combat its dubious distinction as having one of the highest pregnancy and venereal disease rates in the United States, decided that "all public high school students will be eligible to receive condoms from the school nurses."

At first the school superintendent had said that parents who did not want their child to receive condoms could write a note to that effect, and their wishes would be honored. The Washington, DC, public health commissioner, however, had other ideas and overruled the superintendent with this announcement: "Nurses will ignore any notes from parents, will not call any parents if their child asks for a condom, and all visits to receive condoms will be kept confidential. Parents will get a letter informing them of their loss of rights."

There it is! Educators acknowledge they are taking away parental rights!

The commissioner went on to say that "we are the

ones responsible for the health care needs of the children. These are *my* clinics. When a child crosses the door and enters into the nurses' suite, any communication between the child and the nurse is confidential."

Cal Thomas makes this conclusion: "When a child enters the school clinic, he sheds parental authority at the door." As a result, condoms and birth control pills are passed out to elementary children without any moral restraints placed upon them. And if a girl does get pregnant, not to worry, the school nurse will arrange for an abortion — during school hours, of course — take the child to the "clinic" and have this risky medical procedure performed — all without ever notifying the parents or obtaining their permission.

And that's the way our educators want it. They want complete control over our children's minds, bodies — and souls.

"Animal Liberation" for the Gifted

President and Mrs. Clinton themselves have been personally involved in indoctrinating children with liberal ideas that run contrary to the beliefs of most American parents. Thomas Sowell explains that while Bill Clinton was governor of Arkansas, he inaugurated special summer programs called the Arkansas Governor's School for gifted students.

What was the agenda of this summer program? "Ideological indoctrination," writes Sowell.

And how did the leaders of this program indoctrinate Arkansas' best and brightest? Thomas Sowell explains:

> Those Arkansas teenagers were subjected to a one-sided barrage of films, lectures, and readings favoring homosexuality, "animal liberation," pacifism, and a whole string

of other causes dear to the left and far left. One reading in this program challenged the idea of a "male god and a male saviour." Another pictured poverty as being a result of a conspiracy by the American establishment.

Bill Clinton described the school as a "dream come true," and both he and Hillary have lectured in the debased program specifically designed to wear down the moral and ethical values of bright young high school students.

Is this kind of indoctrination working? Absolutely.

The late Allan Bloom, in *The Closing of the American Mind*, writes that the one thing a university professor can be absolutely certain of is that 99 percent of every entering class of freshmen "do not believe there is any such thing as absolute truth."

In an article from *Christianity Today* called "How to Teach: A Blueprint for Moral Right and Wrong; Education in a Pluralistic Age," the question is asked: Are America's public schools graduating a generation of moral illiterates?

One educator, Christina Hoff Summers, who has taught ethics at the university level for 15 years, is convinced that something in the classroom has gone fundamentally wrong. She notes:

> We may be one of the few societies in the world that finds itself incapable of passing on its moral teachings to young people. When it comes to character development and moral education it is as though we've forgotten several thousand years of civilization — the great moral, religious and philosophical traditions.

Summers reached this conclusion after repeatedly coming face to face with a "surprising number of young people who think there's no right or wrong; that moral choices depend on how you feel." While many were decent and kind, she also noted that "they could not justify or defend ethical values." In other words, they had no sense that morality could be normative and absolute.

Summers also saw firsthand how public schools have failed to teach children right from wrong and often retreat from the "traditional task of helping parents to civilize the child." To combat this, she enrolled her child in a private Jewish school where the teaching staff was "not afraid to teach ethics and kindness, where morality was woven into the daily lessons."

Anyone who has children or grandchildren attending public schools today is fully aware of the cruelty that children are allowed to perpetrate on one another in the course of a school day. Name calling, racial slurs, sexual remarks, and even physical abuse are common because there is no adult — on the school bus, in the classroom, on the playground — brave enough to say to a student, "That's wrong!"

These facts should give you an idea of how America's once church-based educational system became the stronghold of secular humanism. But there is more to it than just political appointments and hostile administrators. Before their "coup" could be complete, the educational establishment would have to change not only the thinking of the teachers but the material that the teachers used. It is at this point that the script takes a more sinister turn.

Rewriting American History

In spite of the fact that, by the mid-1800s, the state legislatures had taken control of education, the textbooks used in the schools had not changed. The *McGuffey*

Readers, developed by a frontier preacher, taught biblical and moral virtues using character-building stories. In fact, the public schools were so Protestant in nature that immigrant Catholics started their own parochial schools in the 1890s.

All that began to change in the early twentieth century, when in 1903, "experts" on the Carnegie Foundation Board of Trustees, using tax-free money to the tune of $30 million a year, set out to alter the perception of American history. They planned to do this by hiring scholars to rewrite the history texts used in America's public schools. The history professors, however, refused to cooperate.

That didn't stop the Carnegie trustees and others from the Rockefeller and Ford Foundation who had plenty of tax-free money to throw around. To achieve their purpose, they took a more time-consuming but effective route, which involved funding the education of bright, young collegians who could be molded into their benefactors' form of secular humanism. They sent these students to graduate school and then financed them "to rewrite history" to conform to what is today called "a contemporary view of history."

According to Tim LaHaye, our national heroes, like George Washington, Thomas Jefferson, Benjamin Franklin, and others, were presented, not as men of integrity and virtue, but "as crass human beings who used their public notoriety for personal advantage. . . . Textbooks were purposely changed to include moral indiscretions, suggesting that even Thomas Jefferson had fathered children by one of his slave girls, a report that rests on very dubious evidence."

Garry Wills, in his book, *Under God: Religion and American Politics,* contradicts this distorted view of the Founding Fathers. "There is no evidence of adultery in George Washington's life," Wills writes. "Most scholars deny it in Jefferson's life as well." Still the educational elite insist on trashing the reputations of our Founding Fathers.

In the sixties and seventies, parents began to notice the change in their kids' history books and complained that the texts "gave more space to Joseph Stalin, Mao Tse-t'ung, and Marilyn Monroe than to our Founding Fathers." As a result, an entire generation of young people have been taught false and slanted information that contributes to the educators' humanistic propaganda campaign.

In a study conducted on the content of 60 third and sixth grade textbooks used in 88 percent of American elementary schools, the researchers found 670 stories. Only five of those stories dealt with the era surrounding the founding of America, and none of those five stories were about our Founding Fathers.

What are the five stories about? Not George Washington or Nathan Hale or Paul Revere. In fact, there is no mention of, the great leaders of that time period. Instead, the five stories center around boys and girls — none of whom are well-known — who played some small role in our developing nation.

Forget Religion!

George Roche, president of Hillsdale College, said, "Men without a past are forever children, easily manipulated and enslaved."

No wonder some historians would have us forget Valley Forge, Plymouth Rock, the Boston Tea Party, North Park Church, and the Great Awakening. They would like to erase the legacy left by such great men as Samuel Adams, John Adams, Jonathan Edwards, and Adonirum Judson. They try to cover up and distort the missionary zeal of men like Christopher Columbus, Johnny Appleseed, and David Brainerd. Even Patrick Henry's,

"Give me liberty or give me death," has been deleted from today's "politically correct" textbooks.

Tim LaHaye makes this tragic statement after reviewing over 600 books in the Library of Congress: "If you wish to find a Christian view of our Founding Fathers, you must go back to books written more than 50 years ago."

Dr. Paul C. Vitz, a New York University psychology professor, after examining 60 of the most popular textbooks used in public schools, had this to say: "The most striking thing about these texts is the total absence of the Christian religion in them."

Dr. Vitz went on to point out:

> Other beliefs were mentioned [in these textbooks], Jewish, Amish, Mormon, Catholic faiths, but little or no mention was made of the evangelical Protestants who founded this nation. Secularism is taught in those same textbooks, a life and world view for children and young people that little resembles the one taught in this nation for the first 150 years of its history.

School textbooks don't provide students with historical facts about the influence of the Bible and Christianity upon our nation, but they have no qualms about conveying the false idea that Christianity is out of date. Here is what one textbook had to say about Christianity in American society:

> For a very few, religion can still provide a special sense of embracing, belonging, and selfhood. For most religion is but a Sunday meeting house and nursery school and rec-

reation center which cannot adequately define the entire person.

According to experts Mel and Norma Gabler, the new history, economics, and social study texts emphasize "big brother government, welfarism, and a new socialist global order while putting down patriotism, traditional morality, and free enterprise." Why? The answer is simple. The humanists in education are seeking to bring about the "social realism" that John Dewey and other social reformers have planned for America.

That describes the "new" religion being taught in textbooks today. The Gablers call it "a religion that is hostile to the Judeo-Christian principles upon which American liberty is founded."

How do humanist educators plan to do this? By constantly indoctrinating children with a negative view of religion in history that presents Christians as narrow-minded bigots motivated by hatred and greed.

Patrick Buchanan in his book, *Right from the Beginning,* notes:

> While some of us look back nostalgically and fondly on American history, the liberal and radical now look back and see more that is sinister — slavery and segregation, the despoliation of the environment, the maltreatment of the Native Americans, repression of women, the exploitation of labor.

By imposing this kind of thinking on America's students, humanist educators hope to remove all sympathy for the religious values held by the majority of Americans, past and present. The ultimate goal of these educators is even more frightening: to alienate children from the morals and faith of their parents.

"Children in public schools are under an influence with which the churches cannot compete, and which they cannot counteract," writes Charles Clayton Moore of *Christian Century.* "The public school presents the Church with a generation of youth whose minds have been cast in a secular mold."

Patrick Buchanan makes it clear where we are today in this battle for the minds of our young people:

> Having captured America's public schools and converted them into the parish schools of secular humanism, the new religion that "dare not speak its name" will not readily surrender these unrivaled pulpits for the propagation of the faith, and the secularists make no secret of their intent.

The militant goal of the secularists is summarized in this award winning essay of the American Humanist Association in 1983: "The battle for humankind's future must be waged and won in the public school classroom by teachers who correctly perceive their rule as the proselytizers of a new faith."

Make no mistake about it, they are winning the war. "Allied with the secularists, the media, the academic community," writes Buchanan, "the state and federal education bureaucracies stand shoulder to shoulder while the federal courts shelter their monopoly control."

Toying With National Suicide

In 1992 another assault on America's history began, when the National Endowment for the Humanities set out to write "guidelines" for history textbooks used in grades 5 through 12 in public schools. A grant of $2.2 million of taxpayer money was allocated to the UCLA history center, which devised "The National Standards for United States History."

One suggestion instructs students to "analyze" and "reflect" on such pagan cultures as the child-sacrificing Aztecs and the kingdom of Mali — which have little or nothing to do with early American history.

According to Patrick Buchanan, the guide contains no mention of Paul Revere's ride, Alexander Graham Bell, Thomas Edison, Albert Einstein, the Wright Brothers, Henry Clay, or Daniel Webster.

Aside from simply failing to mention these famous contributors to America's greatness, the new history standards go even further and malign conservative leaders like Ronald Reagan, calling him "a cheerleader for selfishness."

In a further effort to slant the facts, the Ku Klux Klan is presented as a major force in American society and mentioned 17 times. Robert E. Lee, Ulysses S. Grant, and Lincoln's Gettysburg Address are mentioned once.

In a column titled, "Ideologues Hijack U.S. History," Pat Buchanan describes the aggressive agenda of the "politically correct:"

> What is underway here is a sleepless campaign to inculcate in American youth a revulsion toward America's past. . . . The left's long march through our institutions is complete. Secure in tenure, they are now serving up, in our museums and colleges, a constant diet of the same poison of anti-Americanism upon which they themselves were fed.
>
> Ultimate goal: Breed a generation of Americans who accept the Left's indictment of our country, who refuse to defend

her. . . . For any nation to subsidize such assaults upon its history is to toy with suicide.

So where does that leave us today?

With a generation of young people who think Christopher Columbus was a crazed gold digger intent on ravishing the New World of its riches; that our founding fathers were wealthy womanizers and Christians in name only; that America is, was, and always has been a "secular" — even pagan — nation with no Christian foundation.

What effect do such false notions have on our young people? It robs them — and our nation — of its rich Christian heritage, leaving us without a sense of honor and respect for our heroic Founding Fathers.

Abraham Lincoln once said, "The philosophy of education in one generation will be the philosophy of government in the next."

If our future is to bear any resemblance to the past, we must insist on an educational system that tells its students the truth. To do otherwise is to signal the end of the American dream.

7

To Remake a Generation

You have to push as hard as the age pushes against you.
— Flannery O'Connor

It is this loss of the moral sense . . . that constitutes the real challenge to morality in our times. — Will Herberg

In the previous chapter we learned how secular humanistic educators have succeeded in expelling traditional American moral values from our public school systems.

What has been the result?

Tim LaHaye provides the answer: "Since the humanists gained virtual control of education in this country about 50 years ago, not only have academic levels declined, but moral levels have radically deteriorated as well."

Why has this happened? Because secular humanism refuses to take into account the fallen nature of man.

According to LaHaye, humanism "bought from Rousseau the false concept that man is really very good, and that proper education will enable him to make right choices for himself and all mankind."

A stroll through the halls of America's inner city high schools reveals the futility of injecting moral values into sin-hardened hearts.

A recent survey of 13 colleges in the Southeast conducted by the conservative group, Students for America, found that 56 percent of the students polled said that right and wrong is a matter of personal opinion. Only 38 percent said they believe there are absolutes.

Columnist Cal Thomas, who reported these findings, included the story of a theology graduate student at Emory University who said he didn't know if right and wrong is a matter of personal opinion. "One might ask," Thomas writes, "what good it does to study theology if the subject doesn't point the student to an authority higher than his or her own mind."

Thomas then quotes a conservative student who says that today, "attitudes and belief systems among so many college students are not a matter of immorality. Rather . . . it stems from the absence of morals and values . . . amorality."

"If that's the case," the student wonders, "where will we be in another 30 years?"

Good question, especially in light of the fact that in our "amoral" society, the average child, by the end of grade school, has watched 8,000 made-for-TV murders and 100,000 acts of violence.

Is this indulgence in violence having an impact on our society? Yes, according to William J. Bennett's *Index of Leading Cultural Indicators.* He notes that "eight out of 10 Americans can expect to be the victim of violent crime at least once in their lives."

Take the absence of moral education — either at home or in school — and mix it with an irresponsible media that dishes out a constant barrage of gun-toting, happy-go-lucky "terminators" and punch kicking Power Rangers, and we have what we have today — a violent society.

Why Secularism Doesn't Work

Patrick Buchanan in his book, *Right from the Beginning,* suggests there is only one option left if secularist ideology continues to mandate the permanent expulsion of traditional religious teaching from the public schools: "We should probably get on with the building of new prisons. For external force is the only line of defense left."

That is exactly what is happening. The nation's prison population has now topped more than one million for the first time in history — that's almost 400 inmates for every 100,000 people in the United States! Last year alone, 1,400 inmates *a week* were locked up! And most of these convicts — as many as 60 percent — were repeat offenders. To contain the rapid increase of career criminals, the new crime bill has authorized spending $7.9 billion to build new prisons.

That's just the tip of the iceberg. Today, children are killing children. In the last ten years, the number of boys under 18 arrested for murder or manslaughter has more than doubled — from 1,100 to 2,500.

Patrick Buchanan notes why secular humanism will never change anyone's behavior, especially questioning and rebellious teenagers:

> Those who have captured the heights of modern education have no conclusive, convincing answer to the age-old question of youth, "Why not?" Why not casual sex? Why not smoke marijuana? Why not use drugs? Why not steal a pair of Adidas? Why not cheat in class?

We should not be surprised by such attitudes. Our educational system is simply reaping what it has sown. While the biblical story of creation is no longer permitted, Darwin's theory of evolution is taught as fact. Having explained to generations of American young that they are "the descendants of monkeys, we manifest surprise when they emulate their forebears," says Buchanan.

"Even by utilitarian and pragmatic standards," notes Buchanan, "secularism does not work."

If we know their humanistic philosophy doesn't work, why do Americans continue to allow a minority of secularists to determine how and what America's children are taught?

Fortunately, the tide is turning and, according to Buchanan, "more and more Americans are aware that the expulsion of the traditional religious and ethical instruction from the public schools has gone hand in hand with the decline in public education and the collapse of public morality."

So what should the secularists do?

Columnist Cal Thomas has a suggestion for the liberal secularists: "Either own up to the damage they caused in attempting to secularize the culture or shut up, because they have lost the moral authority to be heard."

Time to Step Forward

Who then has the moral authority to change the direction of education in America? I believe that authority belongs to Christian parents and Christian educators. After all, someone has to step forward and take the lead. Why not Christians?

"When the internal constraints of an informed conscience and religious belief no longer bind," writes Buchanan, "then someone's values, someone's beliefs, someone's concept of morality will be transmitted during the education of the child. The only question is whose?"

The democratic process is still alive and well. If Christians don't seize the opportunity to take back our schools, someone else may do it for us.

In the 1950s, there was no "crisis" in American education. Private, parochial, and even public schools succeeded on a fraction of the billions of dollars we spend annually today on public education alone.

The crisis, however, goes beyond "why Johnny can't read" to "why Johnny can't tell right from wrong."

Peter Marshall explains what liberal education does to a child:

> It depersonalizes students to adjust to the technocrats' vision of what they want society to be — where the only virtue is openness and tolerance and the absence of virtue. The National Educational Association wants to "adjust" students into their agenda for restructuring society.

The goal of the educational elite is to "train" students instead of educating them. No wonder secular educators want to rewrite history.

What can we do to protect America's children from this liberal agenda?

Gary Bauer, in his message, "What Happened in America?" makes several suggestions to parents and educators regarding what children should be taught:

> We need to start teaching our children reliable standards of right and wrong again. We need to get over our embarrassment about words like virtue and fidelity and honor and character. . . . We need to be willing to push as hard as the age pushes

against us, and to train our children to do the same, and to resist the siren song that tells them "if it feels good, do it."

We need to teach our children our history; who said, "Give me liberty or give me death;" who said, "I have a dream." We need to teach them what the Great Lady in New York Harbor stands for, and why there was a Berlin Wall and what the forces of liberty were that brought it down.

We need to teach them about Bunker Hill and Concord Bridge and Normandy, and how their liberty was won and nurtured at those places.

And, yes, we even need to teach them about Jonathan and David and Ruth and Naomi. We need to teach them to love the things we love and to honor the things we honor — because nothing less will do.

Remember, a change in the philosophy of education in one generation produces a change in the philosophy of government in the next. If we want to change America, we must develop a new understanding of education.

What, then, should be the objective of education? Is it simply to impart information? No.

"The real point of education," says Peter Marshall, "is to produce leadership. Not just any kind of leadership, but a leadership that is achieved by the formation of character."

Humanist educators cannot produce character because they have no basis on which to build character. Sure, they can make lists of "attitudes" they want children to attain. But any parent who has tried to change a child's attitude knows it is impossible unless the child's heart agrees. And that is something mere "education" can never do.

The Puritans knew the true purpose of education. And what is that? Learning to apply Christian principles to the issues in every area of life. The word education comes from the Latin word, "educare," which means to lead out.

Man cannot create character in children. Only God can do that. In fact, character building is God's business, and it can only be achieved through faith in Jesus Christ. God's purpose is to transform you and me and our children into the people He created us to be.

Peter Marshall notes: "That's the primary issue of your life — not what you are going to *do* for God but who you are going to *become.*"

A Blueprint for Christian Education

In order to help our children build their character, we must first develop a new philosophy of education — a Christian philosophy.

And what should that be?

"The Christian philosophy of education," Marshall proposes, "should be to create an entire generation of adult Christian leaders who will transform America."

How can we achieve such a lofty objective?

First, we need a blueprint from which to build. Fortunately, the most successful form of education the world has ever known originated in America, and we have excellent documentation on its procedures.

How do we know these methods worked? Because colonial New England produced our founding fathers, men who were not only brilliant but mature in Christian character, which is most important.

What made colonial American education unique from all its predecessors? It was based on Judeo-Christian values.

Peter Marshall discovered that Puritan education had as its masthead the verse: "The fear of the Lord is the beginning of wisdom." In other words, true education begins with a relationship with God through Jesus Christ.

Wisdom was their goal — not indoctrination or information. The Puritans were committed to producing adult Christian men and women who could make wise choices and be discerning in their behavior. "It was not just to pack little heads with knowledge," Peter Marshall says.

To achieve this goal, the Puritans had three main elements of their educational process for "creating character and producing leaders" — piety, civility, and learning.

Their first goal, *piety,* was to get the child saved.

Peter Marshall tells why this should be the beginning point for education: "The first step in education has to be regeneration because we are dealing with a sinful, fallen nature. The basic barrier to godly education is sinfulness — not ignorance."

Civility was next because it forms the foundation of civilization.

What is civilization? "It is civility worked into a whole society of people," says Marshall. "Education isn't something that comes from outside to get stuck inside. It's something that God works into people on the inside that gets processed out into their daily life and their mental thinking."

The third element, *learning,* came from the Puritans' strong belief that every child should be educated. This was a radical concept because, in the 1600s, education was provided only for the privileged few — the wealthy and elite. At that time in history, only in the American colonies was every child given the opportunity to learn to read and write.

For the Puritans, education had one main purpose — to teach children to read the Word of God for themselves. As a result, many children learned to read by the age of three.

This is the kind of education our founding fathers received in colonial America — a Christian education that taught them to apply biblical principles to every area of life. As adults, then, they were prepared to write the documents and establish a form of government that would create the greatest nation in the history of the world.

No Surrender!

Now that we have determined what makes up a Christian philosophy of education, what should we do with it? Force it on the educational establishment? Start a Christian school system? Remove all Christian children from public schools and teach them at home?

Patrick Buchanan says we shouldn't throw in the towel and give up on the public educational system:

> Today many Christians, emulating the Catholics of a century ago, are walking away from the public schools and creating their own Christian schools. While these efforts merit sustenance and support through vouchers and tuition tax credits, there is no reason to raise the white flag and forever surrender the public schools. They can be recaptured. Why should a secularist minority rather than a believing majority see its values dominant? Whose schools are they anyway?

To regain control of public education in America, we must insist that the federal government get out of the education business. How can this be done? Buchanan says there is only one way: "The first necessity is to dismantle the monopoly, to decentralize the system, to terminate federal dictation, judicial and bureaucratic."

Who then should be in control? Parents and teachers, as Buchanan explains:

> Parents and teachers, not judges and bu-
> reaucrats, should decide what the school
> shall and shall not teach. Let the character
> of each public school reflect the character
> of the neighborhood and the community in
> which it is located. And let the schools
> compete with one another for the alle-
> giance, the tax dollars, and the vouchers of
> the parents and taxpayers. . . . Surely the
> way to improve education is to enhance the
> classroom authority, the prestige, and the
> pay of the best of the teachers, and to
> provide greater freedom of choice for all
> parents.

School choice. That is the answer. But it has to be more than another "income transfer from taxpayers to an industry that has failed," writes Buchanan. "Monopolies always breed mediocrity. . . . the calcified education industry is in as great a need of competition as was the American auto industry two decades ago."

What if the stranglehold of the National Education Association and government bureaucracy cannot be broken?

Columnist Cal Thomas suggests Christian parents pull their children out of public schools and either establish a superior private school system or teach their children at home. "A superior private system," says Thomas, "would force government schools to change (to make moral instruction an essential component of the curriculum) or go out of business."

Some Selective Civil Disobedience

In his fascinating book, *The Political Mission of the Church,* Billy Falling notes that revivalist George Whitefield fearlessly preached about the Christian's responsibility to be involved in civil government. He said, "We all will answer to God for the deeds done in the flesh," making it clear that civil leaders carried a responsibility given by God. It was to Him they would give account.

According to Falling, Whitefield's teaching on government had three main points. The first was "there are certain fundamental divine laws which a Christian subject must first obey," Falling notes. "However, laws contrary to these principles are open to question and, if necessary, to the breaking of the man-made laws in favor of God's laws."

In light of the fact that "an evil law is no law," according to Thomas Aquinas, Patrick Buchanan makes this rather radical suggestion:

> It is past time for some selective civil disobedience. . . . A national day of prayer conducted "inside" the classrooms of America's public schools by Christian teachers in open defiance of Supreme Court edicts would send a message of political strength the secular city could not ignore. The movement to restore religion to a central role in the education of American children is a cause that is just; it is time that cause found its own Rosa Parks.

In December 1994, the administration of a Colorado high school told the staff and students to eliminate the traditional singing of "Silent Night" from the annual Christmas program. The night of the event, however, as the program ended, one person stood in protest and began to quietly hum the familiar hymn. Soon other students and parents joined in the song, standing one at a time across the auditorium until almost everyone was softly singing the words "Silent Night, Holy Night . . . ."

The administration got the message, and all it took was one person with the courage to initiate "some selective civil disobedience."

A few students in 1991 did just that by meeting to pray around their school's flagpole. They were promptly arrested. Since that time, the Supreme Court has ruled that student-initiated and led prayer is perfectly legal on school property. In recent years, the turnout at "See You At the Pole" has been tremendous — in spite of continued threats from the ACLU — with over one million students participating in 1994.

In 1993, high school principal Bishop Knox of Jackson, Mississippi, convinced that a court ruling on graduation prayer applied to any public setting, decided to test the issue. When students came to him asking if they could say a prayer over the school's public address system, he gave his permission since the request had been approved by an overwhelming vote of the student body.

School officials, however, disagreed and fired Knox. In protest, hundreds of students walked out of class, and, later, thousands of people rallied at the state capitol to support the principal and school prayer.

"I have said to my students numerous times that if you know what is right, then have the courage to do it," Knox, a committed Christian, said in an interview with *Charisma* magazine.

Knox's courage gained him national attention when the incident was publicized in the media through programs like Dr. Dobson's "Focus on the Family" and Phil Donahue's talk show. Finally, after several months, Knox was reinstated to his principal's job, and the Mississippi legislature passed a bill making public prayer permissible in the state's public schools.

Know what is right, and have the courage to do it. What a wonderful — but dangerous — way to live.

"Higher" Education?

In addition to recapturing elementary and high school education, Christians have an even greater medium for producing Christian leaders on the college and university level.

What makes a private Christian college or university different from a state supported institution?

Martin Anderson of the Hoover Institution calls today's secular centers of higher education "mini-socialist states." Why? Because they teach and promote socialist ideas based on radical secular humanism and reap the inevitable results: lowered academic achievement, rampant campus immorality, and extensive cheating.

George Roche spells out the problem:

> Tens of thousands of college seniors do not know when Columbus sailed to the New World, who wrote the Declaration of Independence, or why the Civil War was fought. Businesses rightly complain that they must re-educate college graduates in such basic academic skills as grammar, spelling, and practical math. . . . Despite the dumbing down of the curriculum, pass/fail courses, grade inflation, and all the rest, it is estimated that at least half of all college students cheat.

According to the editors of *The National Review College Guide,* a recent Gallup poll reported that "25 percent of America's college seniors could not tell the difference between the words of Stalin and Churchill; could not distinguish the language of *Das Kapital* from the U.S. Constitution." The Gallup report concluded that 75 percent of the students would have received a "D" or an "F" on the test given to these students about to graduate from college.

These dismal results should not surprise us, especially in light of the fact that the average professor spends only six to nine hours a week in class, and teaching assistants — not faculty — conduct many of the introductory subjects at even the Ivy League schools. That doesn't mean, however, that the universities don't have the money to pay their professors.

In the last 30 years, the total budget for U.S. colleges and universities has grown from $7 billion to $170 billion!

What has been the effect of government subsidy and control?

"The entire system of American higher education," according to Roche, "is academically, morally, and quite literally, going bankrupt." In fact, federally-funded educational institutions are operated "like third-world countries," says Roche, where bureaucracy reigns without accountability, and the students are herded into auditorium-sized "classrooms" like so much cattle.

To make matters worse, all vestige of religious, and especially Christian expression, is considered politically incorrect.

Stephen Carter points out in his book, *The Culture of Disbelief,* that even at the nation's top universities, professors and scholars "fear any expression of religious belief will jeopardize their chances for tenure or promotion." As a result, our institutions of higher learning have reached an absurd point in their "intellectual evolution," says Carter, and go to extreme lengths to divorce themselves "from the basic moral force of religion."

In spite of the fact that "so many of the political issues tearing at the country — abortion, euthanasia, capital punishment, genetic engineering — are rooted in moral and ethical dilemmas," Carter points out, our educational institutions continue to "deny the basis on which matters of morality are decided."

In spite of the absurdities taught on many college campuses, Christians continue to send their children to institutions where their values are demoralized, their minds bombarded with godless ideas, and their souls stripped of all that they once held sacred.

At many schools male and female students spend the night in each other's rooms. I heard about one student whose roommate consistently locked him out of the dorm room at night while he "entertained" his girlfriend. Forced to sleep in the hall or lounge, the abandoned student eventually dropped out of school rather than complain.

Why? Because complaints to administrators about moral issues seldom bring any positive action.

In fact, according to George Roche, at some schools like Pennsylvania State University, "the official policy is that students may not be granted a room change on the grounds that their roommate is a homosexual."

At Cornell University, "resident advisor job applicants have been forced to watch movies of men engaged in sex," writes Roche. Why? In order to evaluate applicants for "homophobic" tendencies.

It is amazing the extremes our institutions of higher learning will go in order to make sure everyone is politically correct according to *their* standards.

Cart Before the Horse?

The Puritans were well aware that university level studies were the medium in which students were able to translate the basics of education into action. In fact, Peter Marshall notes that before a single grammar school was formed in New England, a university had already been established.

Isn't that like putting the cart before the horse? No, the Puritans didn't view education the way we do today.

In colonial times many children were educated at home. After completing their studies, students — as young as 12 — were given a college entrance exam. If they passed, and many of them did, they were accepted into Yale or Harvard or Princeton.

The same process is happening among home-schooled children in America today. Unfettered by a nine-month, 12-year system, home schoolers can move on in their studies as soon as the subjects are mastered. In addition, they have many more opportunities to research topics on their own and develop "life skills" unavailable to classroom-bound children in school settings. As a result, many of them are entering colleges and universities at a younger age than their school-taught counterparts.

The word "university" comes from the idea of one single world view applied to every area of life — a universal education.

Peter Marshall says, "In America, the taproot of university education has been a biblical world view, universally applied to every area of life. *That* is the proper role of a Christian university in America."

Surely there are quality colleges where moral values and conservative ideas are still taught. Yes, plenty of them.

The National Review College Guide, which is subtitled: *America's 50 Top Liberal Arts Schools,* provides a synopsis of schools that offer a quality education with a conservative, and often Christian, foundation. William F. Buckley Jr., in the introduction to the book, notes that the names of the fashionable Ivy League schools are missing. Why? "This is not because you cannot get a good education at Harvard, but because you can graduate from Harvard without getting a good education," Buckley writes. Such is not the case, he says, of the schools in the National Review's list.

Schools like Hillsdale College in Michigan and Grove City College in Pennsylvania and others have freed their institutions from government intrusion by refusing to accept government aid. Why?

George Roche explains that "hundreds of private colleges and universities have learned in recent years that even 'indirect aid,' — that is, aid that goes to their students — makes them 'wards of the state' as far as government is concerned."

So how do these private institutions of higher learning survive? With good fiscal stewardship and private donors they are able to lower tuition and still maintain high academic standards.

Grove City, rated among the top five private schools nationwide, placed ahead of Yale, Princeton, Stanford, and Harvard, in *Money* magazine's "Value Rankings," which measures cost, student-faculty ratio, and SAT scores. With an enrollment of only a little more than 2,000 students, Grove City has to be selective in their admission requirement. The course catalog declares:

> Rejecting relativism and secularism, it fosters intellectual, moral, spiritual and social development consistent with a Christian commitment to truth, morality, and freedom. . . . While many points of view are

examined, the college continues to unapologetically advocate preservation of America's religious, political, and economic heritage of individual freedom and responsibility.

I include this statement to emphasize there are colleges in America today that still maintain high academic standards while at the same time preserving the morals and values that were commonplace on college campuses in the past.

In addition, students who attend these kinds of colleges know they are submitting themselves to a Christian, or at least a conservative, environment in which immorality, crime, and cheating are discouraged and dealt with. As a result, students are able to concentrate on their studies without worrying about whether an all-night beer bash is going on in the dorm room next door.

Cal Thomas writes that "there is a growing awareness among parents and students that in too many institutions of 'higher learning,' the learning is more about lower than higher things."

As a result, parents are searching for schools that will give their college-bound children a quality education without the liberal propaganda that students are often force-fed during their four years of study. Christian parents, especially, want to know that the high price they are paying for their child's higher education will equip them to pursue a successful career and be an effective citizen.

The chief aim of a Christian university, therefore, is to produce adult Christian men and women who can literally change America. Instead of being indoctrinated with humanistic philosophies or trained to be "politically correct," students are educated and encouraged to live by the absolutes of the gospel.

After all, isn't that the kind of education our founding fathers received?

A New Vision for America

As a result of their biblical education, our forefathers created a whole new society. Because they had been educated properly by the Holy Spirit on the equality of human beings under God, the founding fathers understood what no humanist ever can — the biblical source of the rights of man.

Where had they learned about the "rights of man"? Possibly from George Whitefield, whose second teaching on government emphasized the New Testament theme that all men, rich and poor, wise and ignorant, share in the gospel, making all men equal in the fellowship of Christ.

This doctrine of equal rights had strong political implications as it was incorporated into the Declaration of Independence, the Constitution, and the Bill of Rights.

Whitefield's third teaching on government stressed the need for tolerance of various church structures and church creeds. Although this kind of openness to all denominations and sects of the Christian church was rare in his day, Whitefield's only interest was seeing people come to Christ.

The spiritual response to Whitefield's principles "was nearly universal, and the political effect was immense," writes Falling.

What was the effect? People from all levels of society began to realize that they were equal with all others. "The people of America began to see themselves as the Puritans had envisioned it," says Falling, "the instruments of God to be light in a darkened world."

That is the vision that we, as Christians, must recapture. We must begin to see ourselves as revolutionaries who live in a pagan society. At the same time, we must, like the colonists, recognize our God-given rights as individuals.

Samuel Adams said, "The rights of the colonists as Christians may be best understood by reading and carefully studying the New Testament."

We may not be able to remake American society in one generation, but we can remake a *generation* in one generation. Using properly taught biblical values, schools and universities have in the past totally changed the course of American history.

Patrick Buchanan, in *Right from the Beginning*, sums up the challenge before us:

> There is no more important battle shaping up in America than for the hearts and the minds of the next generation. Whether that generation will be traditionalist and Christian or agnostic and atheist; whether its codes of morality and ethics will be based on Judeo-Christian beliefs or the secular nostrums of the moment will be largely determined by America's public schools. And Christianity, too, has the right to compete.

"That is the power of the university," says Peter Marshall. "That is the opportunity, the privilege of a university. That is the calling of an American university in this society. We must once again recover that sense of calling and purpose." How can we do that? Marshall suggests two steps.

First, we must go back and recover the Christian basis for American education.

Second, Marshall says, "We must recover a Christian philosophy of education that will once again have at the core of it a biblical world view that will birth a political movement to restore America. That is God's call."

8

Embracing the World

If you will not have God, . . . you should pay your respects to Hitler and Stalin. —
T.S. Eliot, 1939

Do you think the Church is having a leadership problem?" Richard Halverson was asked.

He replied that the "success orientation of our culture" has infected the principles of church growth, making Christians enamored with numbers.

"If a pastor has a big church building, a big congregation, and a big budget, he is considered successful," Halverson said. "And I can say for myself as a pastor, it is very difficult to resist that kind of motivation. It becomes more and more difficult to draw a line between what is of eternal value and what is only temporal."

That is exactly what happened to the early colonial church in America. The last of Henry Steel Commager's four significant turning points that changed the face of America focuses once again on the Church: "Religion became increasingly a social activity rather than a spiritual experience."

It's hard to believe, but this change in the way God's people viewed the Church's role began to take place before our infant nation was even out of the cradle. The ravages of secularization, which we have discussed in previous chapters, crept into predominantly Puritan New England and eroded its biblical foundation.

How could such god-fearing people allow this to happen? Peter Marshall, writing in his book, *The Light and the Glory,* asks the same question:

> One of the great mysteries that we faced in our search was the question of what finally became of the Puritans? They had seemed to be prospering in every way ... Then like a fire slowly dying down, the spiritual life began to dim, until by the beginning of the 1700s, what had been a blazing light of the gospel of Christ had become only a faint glow from smoldering embers. What had gone wrong?

The Puritans "laid down their Cross," Marshall says, and picked up convenience. What led to this crack in the faith of the Puritans? Marshall explains that a major factor was their inability to instill a love for Christ in the generation that was to follow them:

> They stopped their ears and refused to listen to their ministers, and they ceased to correct and admonish one another and their children, choosing instead greed and privacy, independence and idolatry. The light of Christ grew steadily dimmer. It was attracting hardly any of the children now.

Having raised a generation of unbelievers, the Puritan churches faced a difficult dilemma: What to do about the children of members who had never been converted to Christ themselves, but who now wanted to have their own children baptized in the church?

Peter Marshall explains that the Puritans came up with what was dubbed the "Halfway Covenant," which extended partial membership to unbelieving parents and enabled them to have their children baptized but did not permit them to take holy communion. As a result, church membership was no longer based on a born-again experience but on baptism — a religious ritual that supposedly guaranteed salvation without a personal relationship to Jesus Christ.

Marshall calls it "a Halfway Covenant for half-way committed Christians."

Lost Vision

How things had changed from the total commitment to Christ that led the Puritans' parents to cross an ocean and come to a strange land — risking all for the freedom to worship God.

In his book, *The American Mind,* Commager quotes Mary Ellen Chase, who, writing of Maine during that period, recalled the importance of conversion — or salvation — in those early years:

> Conversion . . . in communities like ours . . . was regarded as a necessary and fearfully important occurrence in one's life, usually undergone in adolescence, but sometimes sadly, yea, *dangerously* deferred until mature years. The conversion of the young in their parishes was the deepest concern of both our ministers, and machinery was each year set in operation by means of which it might be facilitated. This machinery consisted always of the January Week of Prayer and not infrequently also

of revival meetings held whenever the fields seemed especially ripe for the harvest.

Author Ed Howe, makes a similar observation when as he recalls the religion of the New England village of Fairview:

> As soon as a sufficient number of children reached a suitable age to make their conversion a harvest, a revival was commenced for their benefit, and they were called upon to make a full confession with such energy and warned to cling to the Cross for safety with such earnestness that they generally did it, and but few escaped.
>
> If there was one so stubborn that he would not yield from worldly pride, the meetings were continued from Sunday until Monday and kept up every night of the week at the house where the owner of the obdurate heart lived so that he finally gave in. . . . If two or three or four or five would not relent within a reasonable time, the people gave up every other work and gathered at the church in great alarm in response to the ringing of the bell, and there they prayed and shouted the live-long day for the Lord to come down among them.

How seriously did the early Puritans assume the spiritual responsibility for their children! Social reformer Washington Gladden, quoted by Commager, notes that conversion was the main emphasis of the American church: "The conversion of sinners was supposed to be the preacher's main business . . . the immense importance of saving men . . . overshadowed all other interests."

Today, however, the pastor and the congregation often find themselves caught up with business other than evangelism. Fundraising efforts, building committees, political action groups, square dancing, bingo, arts and crafts. Sometimes it's difficult to tell the Church from other non-profit institutions. Somewhere along the line the Church in America lost its vision.

A Different Gospel

Over the years there emerged in this country a different gospel that came to be known as the "social gospel."

William Dean Howells, an acute observer of the religious scene who is quoted in *The American Mind*, details how this change from a gospel of salvation to a social gospel took place within the Church.

> Religion there had largely ceased to be a fact of spiritual experience, and the visible church flourished on condition of providing for the social needs of the community. It was practically held that the salvation of one's soul must not be made to be depressing, or the young people would have nothing to do with it. Professors of the sternest creed temporized with the sinners and did what might be done to win them to Heaven by helping them to have a good time here. The Church embraced and included the world.

The Church embraced and included the world! Why, I wonder, hadn't the world "embraced and included" the Church? If Christians had been having an "eternal" impact on their culture, surely it would have affected society in positive ways. Instead, the Church took on the ways of the world, and both suffered as a result.

The American notion, as Spanish philosopher George Santayana put it, was that religion "should be disentangled as much as possible from history and metaphysics, and made to rest honestly upon one's own feelings, on one's indomitable optimism and trust in life."

Commager writes about Washington Gladden of Springfield, Massachusetts, who became the spokesman for socialized Christianity. Although Gladden had been brought up as a strict, conservative Christian, he came under the influence of Horace Bushnell, who regarded Christianity as "a fellowship of love" and the Church "as a social agency."

Gladden considered evangelism to be "almost wholly individualistic" because "it constantly directed the thoughts of men to the consideration of their own personal welfare." In other words, he thought Christians should be more concerned about others than their own personal salvation.

Dr. Richard Land of the Southern Baptist Christian Life Committee says that "the idea of a social gospel and a spiritual gospel is contrary to the teachings of Jesus and the Bible as a whole. "There's only one gospel, and it is a whole gospel for whole people."

Dr. Land continues:

> It is blasphemous to seek to feed the hungry and not tell them about the Bread of Life. Or to clothe the naked and not tell them about the whole armor of God or to seek to house the homeless and not tell them that in our Father's house are many mansions. But it is also blasphemous . . . to seek to minister to the spiritual needs of the people and to neglect or be insensitive to their physical plight. We are to do both.

"We can't have a dichotomy between revival and reform," says Dr. Land. "We have to have both." Why? He explains:

> We've got to have a revival that changes the heart of men and of women that will then impel us out into the public marketplace of ideas to seek and defend those who can't defend themselves — the unborn, the homeless, those who are being molested as sexual objects as children and teenagers, those who are being denied health care in their illnesses or in their terminal years and are being allowed to die before their natural time.

A true social gospel is just that — the combination of meeting the physical and material needs of people while offering them the hope and freedom that only the truth of the gospel can provide.

Out of the Closet and Into Your Face!

Commager explains the liberal, social mind set that finally took over reformer Washington Gladden's thinking:

> Neither Darwinism nor the Higher Criticism embarrassed him; he welcomed them rather as allies which freed Christianity from literalism and enabled the Church to reclaim those who had been affronted by its irrationality.

Isn't that the same verbiage being bantered about today by social reformers who criticize fundamental Christians? "Bigot" is their favorite word, and many religious leaders who have preached the social gospel for decades are caving in to the demands of gay and lesbian activists.

"The revisionists present it as a simple issue," writes Stephen L. Jones in *Christianity Today.* "The Church has evolved in rejecting slavery, racism, and sexism and now it is time to stop its most deeply entranced bigotry: homohatred, heterosexism, and homophobia."

Mel White, who at one time was a ghost writer for several leaders of the religious right, including Pat Robertson, Jerry Falwell, and others, has recently "come out of the closet" and declared himself to be a homosexual.

Dennis Wheeler, in quoting Mel White, reveals how gay activists hope to squelch religious objections to the homosexual "lifestyle":

> We have gone underground, and we have people in every one of the religious right's organizations. We're on their mailing lists. We're reading everything they're putting out. We think the words from their mouths trickle down into violence. And when our evidence reaches a critical mass, we're going to use the best attorneys in this country to bring a class action suit in 50 states to have it stopped. I know them better than anybody knows them; so this war I'm declaring is personal. They're my friends, my enemy.

That statement is mild compared to other tactics being used by the gay community. The book *When the Wicked Seized the City*, by Chuck and Donna McIlheny, recounts the attempt by homosexuals to silence the voice of protest in San Francisco. Like Lot, Christians who have the courage to proclaim the truth of God's Word concerning homosexuality have been viciously attacked. Their churches have been desecrated and their wives and children threatened.

Dennis A. Wheeler tells us what is at stake:

> The homosexual lobby has aimed its cannon directly at the Christian Church. It has done so because the church safeguards the moral ethic that condemns homosexuals as wretched perverts who *must* change their behavior or suffer severe consequences.
>
> Mel White's plan to use the courts of law to silence Christendom reveals the intention of the homosexual movement: the complete and total overthrow of the Christian moral order under which western civilization has existed and flourished for hundreds of years.

F. LaGard Smith, in his book, *Sodom's Second Coming,* points out the almost schizophrenic thinking of gay activists: "In the gay rights' assault against the American culture, no citadel is more coveted than the church. Getting the church's imprimatur on the homosexual lifestyle would be the ultimate stamp of legitimacy; nothing is more important than that."

"Gay" Christians?

Pastor Jack Hayford, in a message about homosexuality, quoted a psychiatrist from UCLA, who said:

> The term virgin has become outmoded. Aberrant sexual behavior is everywhere. Therefore, researchers regret society's moral stance that sexual aberration is unnatural; and they regret the repressive so-

cial action that results. Society's condemnation may be all that is pathologic, not the behavior itself.

In other words, the onus is on the opposition. The person who finds homosexual conduct abhorrent, unbiblical, unhealthy, or wrong is the one with the problem.

Lesbian Presbyterian minister Jane Spahr has been quoted as saying: "There are more and more of us feeling wonderful about who we are. We don't buy into the myth of what society puts on us. I love being lesbian, love the integration of sexuality and spirituality; it's important that our spirituality is eclectic; that it is open; that whatever you are I will walk with you."

Stephen L. Jones, writing in the July 19, 1993, issue of *Christianity Today*, concludes that the apologists for the "gay Christian" movement claim to be "staunchly within the Christian tradition," but at the same time these so-called "revisionists terribly distort biblical sexual ethics."

Jones mentions one such revisionist — Presbyterian minister, Chris Glasser, who has written a book about new sexual ethics titled *Come Home: Reclaiming Spirituality and Community as Gay Men and Lesbians.*

Glasser believes that *fidelity* does not mean "being sexually exclusive and monogamous." Fidelity really means only keeping your promises. "So if a gay Christian companion promises to have only five other lovers per year," Jones concludes, "he is being faithful if he stays within those limits."

Episcopal biblical scholar, William Countryman, in his book *Dirt, Greed, and Sex,* also proposes a "theology" that allows for homosexual practice, but he goes further and also makes prostitution and sex with animals a legitimate option for Christians!

At the same time that these "alternative lifestyles" are being promoted, heterosexual marriage is ridiculed and has even been labeled as a practice that "enslaves women." At least that's what Episcopal ethicist Carter Heyward writes in her book, *Touching Our Strength.* Jones notes that Heyward calls instead for "loving, sexual friendships" that need not be limited "to only one person or only one sex."

Revised Theology

Those who call themselves Christians and profit from writing about "liberation" theology are actually tightening the chains of homosexuality more firmly around their brothers and sisters. They remind me of the words of the Lord, spoken through Jeremiah the prophet:

> "Because from the least of them to the greatest of them, everyone is given to covetousness; And from the prophet even to the priest, everyone deals falsely. They have also healed the hurt of My people slightly, saying, 'Peace, peace!' when there is no peace. Were they ashamed when they had committed abomination? No! They were not at all ashamed; nor did they know how to blush. Therefore they shall fall among those who fall; At the time I punish them, they shall be cast down," says the Lord (Jer. 6:13-15).

In spite of such warnings, the "prophets and priests" of the new social gospel continue their deceit.

An article in *The Christian Century* notes that "local Episcopal, Catholic, Jewish, and Methodist groups drafted resolutions, later passed by their national assemblies, regarding patient services and congregational education about AIDS. These resolutions also decry homophobia, especially among religious groups."

Such "revised theology" does not view homosexuality as "inherently sinful" and, according to the article, encourages "strong gay relationships" rather than condemnation of "homosexual activity."

The magazine also puts a positive spin on the AIDS epidemic, noting that the disease has led "religious groups to a more positive stance on homosexuality." These examples are then cited:

> Catholics and Jews are fighting AIDS related discrimination, Episcopalians are pushing for a gay marriage ceremony, and some Presbyterians and members of the United Church of Christ are urging the ordination of self-avowed homosexuals.

In his book, *Sodom's Second Coming,* F. LaGard Smith tells about Robert Williams, the first openly gay priest to be ordained in the Episcopal Church. Although he claimed to have accepted Christ as a boy in his hometown Baptist church, as an adult Williams attended dozens of different churches until he fell in with New Agers and gay religious groups.

In his search to find acceptance for his homosexuality he finally discovered "high church" Anglo-Catholic worship. Here is how Robert Williams explains away his deviant behavior:

> The point is not really whether or not some passage in the Bible condemns homosexual acts. The point is that you cannot allow your moral and ethical decisions to be determined by the literature of a people

whose culture and history are so far removed from your own. You must dare to be
iconoclastic enough to say, "So what if the
Bible does say it, who cares?"

In an effort to downplay the first chapter of Romans,
where homosexuality is called "unnatural," Williams
rejects the authority of Scripture by equating God's Word
with that of man's:

Perhaps Paul *is* condemning homosexuality in this passage, or at least labeling it as
"unnatural" (which is not exactly the same
thing as calling it sinful), but the bottom
line for you is, So what? Paul was wrong
about a number of other things, too. Why
should you take him anymore seriously
than you take Jerry Falwell or Anita Bryant
or Cardinal O'Conner?

To gain public legitimacy for the homosexual lifestyle,
Williams and other homosexuals must first reduce God's
Holy Word to a point where it is open to negotiation and
which, according the them, they can accept or reject.

Yale historian John Boswell, writing in *Christianity,
Social Tolerance and Homosexuality,* blames the church's
antipathy toward homosexuals on "misinterpretations of
Scripture." He says the reference to homosexuality as an
"abomination" in Leviticus is a translation of the Hebrew
word that really means something that is ritually unclean
for Jews, like eating pork.

Boswell stretches the point when he claims that
Sodom and Gomorrah were destroyed not because of
their citizens' homosexuality but because of their lack of
hospitality to angels!

Why all this hermeneutical meandering? Their goal

is simple: to change the Word of God so they can feel better in their sin.

Stephen L. Jones, writing in *Christianity Today,* notes: "There are only two ways one can neutralize the biblical witness against homosexual behavior: by gross misinterpretation, or by moving away from a high view of Scripture."

Some church theologians, it seems, have applied both methods to arrive at their new acceptance and actual "celebration" of the homosexual lifestyle.

The Ultimate Depravity

Richard Halverson, in his book *The Timelessness of Jesus Christ,* summarizes a report in *Christianity Today* about a group of Protestant clergymen who had formed a Council on Religion and Homosexuals "to establish dialogue between homosexuals and the religious community."

One of the group's main goals was to get a law passed that does not discriminate against homosexuals. To raise money for the project the group helped sponsor a benefit ball for the homosexual "cause." Halverson describes what happened: "Police broke up the ball and arrested five men and a woman. Two of the men were charged with lewd conduct on the dance floor after being officially warned against public intimacies."

What did the ministers, who were in attendance, do? They protested the police intrusion! Not only did they condone the display of outright homosexual behavior in pubic, but they defended it!

That reminds me of a verse from the first chapter of Romans, which condemns not only those who practice wickedness but those who approve and condone the acts of the wicked.

Who, knowing the righteous judgment of
God, that those who practice such things
are worthy of death, not only do the same
but also approve of those who practice
them (Rom. 1:32).

Why are homosexuals so bent on public display of
their lewd sexual acts? Halverson explains the reason:

They want to see it on the screen, on the
stage. They want to read it in books, they
want to see it in advertising. It is not
enough to do it, but they want to see it done.
They take pleasure in it, they are entertained by it. There is nowhere else to go.
This is the dead end.

Halverson writes that "this build-up of degeneration"
is "the ultimate in depravity" when the "vicarious enjoyment of lust" becomes "entertainment." That's why pornography is so popular. "Pleasure in such things is consis-
tent with a godless existentialism," says Halverson.

Surely the Church would not become involved in
such godless activities? I wish that were true.

Another news item in that same issue of *Christianity
Today* reported that the Judson Memorial Baptist Church
in New York's Greenwich Village had a dance program.
That doesn't sound so bad until we read that the program
"included a number in which a man and a woman, both
naked, moved across the stage in face-to-face embrace."

That took place in a Baptist church named in honor of
America's first foreign missionary, Adonirum Judson!

I know there are many Bible-believing Baptist pastors who were as shocked as I was to read this report, but
this approval of homosexual activity has spread beyond
the Greenwich Village church.

Some churches are now ordaining homosexuals and permitting them to lead gay churches. "When I see gay rights activists," writes F. LaGard Smith, "being ecclesiastically blessed by the spiritually emasculated products of some of our nations' religious seminaries fraudulently cross-dressing as ministers of the gospel, I want to overturn the pseudo-scholarly tables of these pandering flesh merchants and throw them out of God's holy temple!"

It is not difficult to understand Smith's outrage. I recall my own feelings when I visited a homosexual "congregation" in which gays and lesbians, tears streaming down their cheeks, sang the chorus, "We Are Standing on Holy Ground," knowing that their lifestyle flies in the face of a Holy God who calls their conduct an abomination.

Spiritualizing Homosexuality

An article in the *Christian Century* quotes people who work with those dying of AIDS as saying that "much of the psychological suffering of AIDS patients is caused by a moral code that condemns homosexual activity."

It is not just the unchurched who are making such comments in an effort to blame Christians; such thinking is rampant within established denominations.

Some time ago, I sat in the sanctuary of the First Baptist Church in Seattle, Washington, and heard the pastor, Dr. Rodney R. Romney, preach that "the time has now come for the Church to call itself into judgment."

What did he mean? That Christians who hold to the teachings of the Word of God have contributed to the AIDS disease by alienating homosexuals because of our divisive, old-fashioned "bigoted" message.

"AIDS is not a homosexual disease," declared Dr. Romney. "In this country it is resident in the homosexual community," and, he says, "because of that we are being forced to examine our beliefs about homosexuality."

His "re-examination" led him to conclude that "homosexuality is selected by certain biological factors" over which, he says, "people have no real choice." He then rationalizes that homosexuality should be "celebrated" since it is "a part of God's intention."

In order to refute the teaching of the Word of God, Romney ridiculed people "who drag out three or four passages from the Old Testament" and "one or two from the New Testament." Then to the laughter of his audience, he said, in speaking of the apostle Paul, "bless his dear, narrow heart."

The pastor concluded by remarking that Jesus chose to say nothing about homosexuality at all except, "Whosoever will may come."

At that point, I thought of our Lord's solemn warning: "Enter by the narrow gate; for wide is the gate and broad is the way that leads to destruction" (Matt. 7:13).

May God spare us from the judgment that must surely come when not only the nation but the Church tolerates and sanctions the abomination of homosexuality.

Who Knows Better?

What about mounting "evidence" suggesting certain persons are born gay? Stephen Jones, writing in the July 19, 1993 issue of *Christianity Today,* puts this question in perspective:

> The existence of inclinations, orientations, or preferences have little to do with God's moral call upon our lives. Social science is finding many powerful factors that shape character and influence morally laden choices. Alcoholism, anxiety-proneness, ill-temperedness, and even the propensity

to violence are made more likely by the presence of genetic and family variables. Is it unfair, then, for God to hold up sobriety and moderation, trust and faith, self-control and patience, restraint and respect, as moral values?

No. Because God is the Maker, the one who sets the design. And though God is perfectly just, He never promised to be fair by human standards. We are saved by grace, but in the race that Paul talks about — the race to press on to the high calling of Christ — some of us start further back in the pack than others, further back from the ideal. But that does not make the goals that God ordains illegitimate or nonbinding.

In His Word, God has given Christians two solid reasons to reject homosexuality as a "legitimate moral option." These reasons are as old as Adam and Eve and as exciting as the Song of Solomon and have been the foundation of every successful society since the beginning of time.

What are these reasons? They are summed up in two words: marital sex. God made sex to be a loving act between a husband and wife for their own enjoyment and for the procreation of children. Sex without marriage leads to sorrow, guilt, and perversion. Marriage without sex produces loneliness, depravation, and divorce.

God knew what He was doing from the day He made man and woman. Why should we think we know better?

Still, some Christians continue to look to the world and the mind of man for life's answers. Let us not be among them.

The Church in America must stop embracing the

world and concentrate on spiritual revival. With revival will come the much-needed social reform our nation so desperately needs.

"America was born," avowed President Coolidge, "in a revival of religion. Back of that revival were John Wesley, George Whitefield, and Francis Asbury."

It cannot be denied that the Wesleyan revival spared England a blood bath similar to that which tore the heart out of France during the French Revolution. That great spiritual awakening also led to the enactment of much-needed child labor laws and prison reform.

When our young nation was threatened by unbelief and apostasy, a move of the Spirit of God stanched the hemorrhage and brought us back to our senses. Every revival that has taken place in our nation's history has had three parts: a call to repentance, a renewal of the Holy Spirit's working in individual personal lives, and social change.

Fires Grown Cold

A revival movement often results in the establishment of a church and maybe a denomination, and for a period of time there is growth, evangelism, and outreach. Then somewhere along the line, individual churches are consolidated into structured organizations, and the zeal drains from once-alive congregations. It has happened time and time again.

With hearts grown cold, the church needs revival, but the very idea of calling in a fired-up evangelist brings objections from those now too sophisticated for a week of knee-bending and tear-shedding repentance at the altar.

Whatever became of revival? Whatever happened to the revivalists?

When I was a boy, every church had at least two week-long revival meetings a year. Everything was put

186 • *Come Home America*

aside, and everyone came — the young and the old. Night after night they came. Each service ended with people thronging the altar, weeping tears of repentance and joy in the presence of the Lord.

Many revivals were open ended. It was not uncommon to find it necessary to extend the revival for another week. "God is moving here, and we can't stop now," the pastor would say.

Most denominations began as revival movements. My church was born in revival. There were no exceptions. We knew little in those days of church planting as a science. There were no seminars on church growth. We gathered in store fronts, rented halls, tents — too often patched and repaired — in brush arbors and on the streets.

I was saved in such a setting. Sitting in a great camp tabernacle, I heard the Holy Spirit speak to me; and the first time God called, I came.

I'll never forget my pastor father standing at the end of a long, home-made altar, lined with kneeling sinners who had come "Home"! Dad captured the scene with his camera; it was a picture to remember.

I recall as a boy how we were warned about becoming "just another denomination." We debated the merits or demerits of establishing a youth department or a women's ministry. We feared the trap of organization and routine.

My church, the church of my father, has become a denomination. We have moved on to become institutionalized.

What is wrong with that? Nothing, maybe. The problem is in keeping the machinery operating. The pastor must be preacher, administrator, counselor, money raiser, psychologist, innovator, builder, a man of the people — and a man of God.

I see another problem that exists in many churches. In an attempt to meet the needs of people, the church has fragmented families. In too many cases, the youngsters never see the sanctuary until they are 10 or 11 years of age. I'm not opposed to children's programs or graded lessons, but it is important for children to worship with their parents, at least occasionally.

Three brothers from my family are preachers, partly because we watched tears flow down Mother's face until we came to believe that little matters unless there is eternity in it.

Why I Weep

When a congregation sets aside a time to seek God in a revival, everyone — from the church leadership to the children — can come together and sit under the gospel preaching of the visiting evangelist. But things have changed.

Today the evangelist is invited to a week of meetings and preaches to a Sunday morning crowd. Half or fewer of the congregation attend in the evening. A few faithful members appear on Monday and Tuesday nights.

On Wednesday night, as the evangelist finishes his sermon and leaves the auditorium, he bumps into more people than he's seen since Sunday morning. And he wonders: Do these people know we're in revival? Are these church leaders grooming the youngsters who will someday become deacons, Sunday school teachers, choir members — or pastors? Do these "Christian" children know who we are, where we came from, and the price that was paid for our "success"?

I know that customs change and that no method is sacrosanct. I have no hankering for hard wooden benches, clapboard tabernacles, used hymnals, borrowed chairs, or starvation wages. But my soul thirsts for the living God, for a move of the Holy Spirit that will sweep aside lethargy and formalism and establish the divine presence in our midst.

When I look at what is happening in the world today and hear the warnings from educators, politicians, and scientists, I want to ask, "Where is the Church?"

I am not a prophet, but I am the son of a prophet. When Dad signed his letters "For Christ and Souls," it was more than a signature, it was a passion.

I am no prophet, but I weep for the 10 year old who seldom hears his pastor preach. I weep for the teenager who has never seen a move of God. I weep for young parents working two and three jobs to pay the bills. I weep for the church that has settled in for the status quo.

I'm not suggesting that we remain mindlessly wedded to the "old ways." We might, however, ask what we have gained by abandoning some of them. It is easy to remember the good while forgetting the bad — there was plenty of that. I *am* appealing, however, for a gospel that challenges young and old alike to have a personal, vital relationship with the living God.

> Oh, breath of life,
>   come sweeping through us;
> Revive Thy church with life and power.
> Oh, breath of life,
>   come cleanse, renew us,
> And fit Thy church to meet this hour.

This must be our prayer for the Church in this last decade of the twentieth century.

9

Coming Apart at the Seams

The Massachusetts Supreme Court ruled by a six to one margin that a man could not award goldfish as prizes in games of chance. It reasoned that such practices "dull the humanitarian feeling of prize winners." The same court made Medicaid funding of abortions mandatory throughout the state. — Paul B. Fowler

A society that does not bow down to worship Almighty God," notes Peter Marshall, "begins to literally come apart because it cannot deal with the tremendous burden of sin. Individually and corporately, we start to come apart."

The evidence is all around us. Our nation is coming apart at the seams.

Peter Marshall, in his book, *The Light and the Glory,* notes the consequences of a culture that has left God out of the picture:

> American families seem to be unraveling;
> a divorce rate that was approaching one
> marriage in two when two generations ago

divorce had been almost unheard of. The sudden prevalence of child abuse, which had been even rarer. The wholesale abdication of parents from the traditional roles of leadership, and the determination of each member of the family to achieve independence — as much and as soon as possible.

Richard C. Halverson, in his book, *The Timelessness of Jesus Christ: His Relevance in Today's World*, quotes from a 1965 issue of *Time* magazine, which reported the thinking of "progressive" church leaders:

The twentieth century sexual revolution directly challenges Christianity's teachings — biblical teachings against fornication and adultery. As an alternative, they propose an ethic based on love rather than law, in which the ultimate criterion for right and wrong is not divine command but the individual's subjective perception of what is good for himself and his neighbor in each given situation.

"In other words," Halverson says, "I am my own law. I decide what is right for me, you decide what is right for you." In fact, church leaders were quoted in the *Time* article as saying, "No sexual relationship should be absolutely condemned by the church."

The result? Rampant sexual promiscuity, which, according to Peter Marshall, "we scrambled to accommodate through legalized abortion, permissive sex education, and evermore effective birth preventatives."

Joseph Fletcher of the Episcopal Theological School said, "One enters into every decision-making moment armed with the wisdom of the culture but prepared in one's freedom to suspend and violate any rule except one must as responsibly as possible seek the good of one's neighbor."

How can the wisdom of a reprobate "culture" be expected to act "responsibly" when there are no guidelines or absolutes to determine what is right and what is wrong? That's why in America today, we call "evil good and good evil" (Isa. 5:20).

As a result, our nation has moved toward spiritual and moral anarchy while everyone does what is "right in his own eyes" (Prov. 21:2).

The "Right" to Kill

Halverson makes the point that even the human rights movements, although correct in principle, "have been affected by anarchy and narcissism." In fact, one leader defines civil rights as a "blank check, payable on demand."

What about civic responsibility? Halverson points out that "rights without responsibility do not beget freedom, but lead ultimately to chaos and bondage . . . irresponsibility is not a solution."

Nowhere is this more true than in the matter of "abortion rights."

Every 20 seconds, a woman demands her "rights," and a baby is killed in its mother's womb. Whether the infant is burned with saline, ripped limb from limb, or sucked out in tiny pieces, he or she experiences excruciating pain.

No matter how much they try to deny it — to themselves and others — every abortion doctor knows a baby suffers when it is killed in the womb. In fact, according to a recent survey of 1,000 abortionists, 38 percent expressed moral misgivings about the abortion procedure itself.

Since 1973, we have been aborting between 1.5 and 1.6 million American babies every year. That's 4,400 babies a day — every day, seven days a week for almost 22 years. One out of every three babies conceived dies without seeing the light of day. Those 30 million murdered Americans make up one-third of a generation.

Dr. Richard Land of the Southern Baptist Christian Life Committee, in a sermon titled, "Sanctity of Life — Taking a Stand," puts abortion statistics into perspective for today:

> The first 1.5 million of these babies would be sophomores in college or in their second year in the work force. The second 1.5 million would be freshmen in college, or in their first year in the work force, with productive lives ahead of them. The third 1.5 million would be seniors in high school preparing for graduation and either going on to college or entering the work force, with a lifetime of productivity ahead of them.
>
> Boys and girls, young men and young women, that we'll never know because we as a nation have been practicing child sacrifice. We've been sacrificing our children on the pagan altars of social convention, material well-being, and career advancement.

Patrick Buchanan notes that "the equivalent of the population of Australia has been sliced up in the womb and sucked out in a country that endlessly lectures the world on human rights."

Who Is to Blame?

How did this happen? Where were we when the death

sentence for one-third of our population was handed down?

This report from *Newsweek* magazine provides the historical setting for one of the most diabolical deeds ever committed in the history of mankind:

> It wasn't even the biggest news story of the day. On January 22, 1973, before a packed gallery, the Supreme Court of the United States declared that a woman has a constitutional right to an abortion. But that seven to two decision written by Justice Harry Blackman played second fiddle in the headlines to another event. Lyndon Johnson, the former president, was dead. A day later, a cease-fire in Vietnam was announced. That pushed *Roe v. Wade* off the front pages altogether. LBJ went out with an impressive funeral, and the war drew to a close, but the courts' action turned out to be a trembler that would transform the landscapes of American society and politics.

The Supreme Court somehow "found a previously undiscovered right to privacy in the Constitution of the United States," Dr. Land notes, "leading them to abolish virtually all of the existing laws in all of the 50 states regulating abortion." Abortion in the first two trimesters of pregnancy was now a "right."

The court left it up to the states to regulate abortion in the last trimester, when in all likelihood the child could live outside the womb with medical assistance. In some states, however, a full-term baby can be murdered up until the moment it is "born." In fact, some abortions are performed using Cesarean section after which the newborn baby is discarded into a bucket as so much "trash."

Dr. Francis Schaeffer, in a message titled, "A Christian Manifesto," tells about an article in *Newsweek* that detailed the baby in the womb: "The first five or six pages show conclusively what every biologist has known all along . . . that human life begins at conception. . . . You flip the page and there is a big black headline, 'But Is It a Person?' "

Then Dr. Schaeffer reads the last sentence from the *Newsweek* article: "The problem is not determining when actual human life begins but when the value of that life begins to outweigh other considerations such as the health or even the happiness of the mother."

How can the life of a tiny, innocent, growing baby be of lesser value than the "happiness" of the mother? Who in their right mind could ever come up with such an idea? What kind of people would allow children to be regularly executed so the "mother" can be happy?

Patrick Buchanan, writing in 1990, explains the collective guilt that we as Americans share for this travesty:

> While the Supreme Court may have given its *nihil obstat* to the slaughter of the innocent, the federal government did not mandate those 18 million deaths. We the people did. For those who believe in the sanctity of all human life, the abortuaries of the West are the free-world terminals for the trains that left earlier this century for destinations like Vorkuta and Kolyma, Treblinka, and Auschwitz — killing fields founded on the Orwellian principle that while all human beings are equal, some are more equal than others.

"The Supreme Court is not the supreme authority for

Christians," Dr. Land reminds us. "Let's remember that the Supreme Court can be wrong. The Supreme Court was wrong in 1857, when it said, in the Dred Scott decision that slaves aren't people." He explains:

> The Supreme Court can't tell us what's right and wrong. They can only give us nine lawyers' opinions about what's legal and what's illegal, and that's a far cry from what's right and what's wrong.

Still, we have to live with the results — millions of dead babies who don't even receive a proper burial but are flushed down drains, tortured in fetal experimentation, or ground up as ingredients for facial creams. Such is the horrible fate of this unprotected segment of tiny people in our society.

How far we have fallen.

The Stopper Is Out!

Our forebears were certain about one thing — man is a sinner by nature and without that sin nature there would be no need for government. The notion that man is the measure of all things, that man can save himself, that man alone and unaided by a God can usher in Utopia always leads to death. During the French Revolution, such thinking resulted in the Reign of Terror and the deaths of thousands — it is either the guillotine or the cross.

In America, it started with abortion, and it may not end until every non-productive citizen — from the Downs Syndrome infant to the elderly Alzheimer's patient — is eliminated by a society that worships man instead of God.

H. Richard Niebuhr, the American theologian, described the Christianity captured by its culture like this: "A god without wrath, brought man without sin into a kingdom without judgment, through the ministrations of a Christ without a Cross."

Dr. C. Everett Koop, speaking at a seminar titled, "Whatever Happened to the Human Race?" said, "When I graduated from medical school the idea was, 'How can I save this life?' But for a great many of the medical students now it's not, 'How can I save this life,' but, 'Should I save this life?' "

Francis Schaeffer makes this profound observation: "Once you begin chipping away, in the medical profession, at the intrinsic value of human life founded on the Judeo-Christian concept that man is unique because he is made in the image of God . . . take it away, and . . . the stopper is out of the bathtub for all human life."

Dr. Richard Land, in his message, "Sanctity of Life — Taking a Stand," tells this story:

> On Palm Sunday, 1982, a little baby boy was born in Bloomington, Indiana. He's known to American legal history as Baby Doe. He had Downs Syndrome, which meant that he was going to have anywhere from mild to very severe mental retardation. He also had a digestive problem. His digestive system was not connected.
>
> The doctor said, "We can take care of that, through an operation, but there is another option. You could deny permission to connect his digestive system because, after all, he is going to be mentally retarded, and he might not meet your quality of life standards to live."
>
> These parents chose the latter option, so Baby Doe was put in the back of the nursery, and instructions were placed on him that he was to receive no food or no

water because he could not digest them. And for four days Baby Doe cried because, like every little boy, he needed food and he needed water. Several of the nurses requested to be assigned to other duties because they could not stand to listen to the pitiful cries of this little baby boy.

On Thursday the Attorney General of Indiana found out what was going on. He went immediately to the Indiana Supreme Court and sought to get an injunction, saying that even a condemned criminal had the right to a stay of execution, pending appeal of his case. On Good Friday, as he prepared to fly to Washington, DC, to plead his case before the Supreme Court of the United States, Baby Doe died.

I believe that Baby Doe is in the arms of Jesus. His ordeal is over. Ours continues because the Supreme Court of the United States of America on two separate occasions in two separate cases has upheld the right of parents to do exactly what Baby Doe's parents did.

In hospitals in the United States of America today, there are babies who are being allowed to die after they are born because they don't meet their parents' standards for normalcy.

Former Surgeon General Dr. Jocelyn Elders said in testimony before Congress, that abortion had "improved the health of the country." When asked to defend this astounding statement, she appealed to studies that showed after the *Roe v. Wade* decision the number of children being born in America with Downs Syndrome and who were mentally retarded had dropped dramatically.

Why was this? Because they were being aborted before they were ever born. According to the Surgeon General, mental retardation is a death sentence — or should be.

How does she, like so many others, justify her stand on abortion?

According to Dr. Francis Schaeffer, "liberal theology is only humanism using theological terms. . . . So it shouldn't surprise us when liberal theologians, or even people who belong to liberal denominations, come down on the side of easy abortion and infanticide. It follows as night to day. We shouldn't be surprised that the liberal theologians have been no help."

Then Dr. Schaeffer asks this pointed question: "But where have the Bible-believing Christians been?"

Where We Are Headed

Dr. Richard Land remembers the case of Nancy Krusane:

> For the first time in American history, the courts of America ruled on the giving of food and water to a comatose patient — not brain dead, not on a heart-lung machine, just comatose. Nancy had a swallowing reflex but, since she was unconscious, she couldn't get up and get herself a glass of water or something to eat.
>
> She was in a persistent vegetative state from which people have recovered, but the feeding tube was removed from Nancy Krusane. Eleven days later she expired from dehydration and malnutrition.

She wasn't even cold yet, when some of those who had advocated that course of action said, "You know dying of dehydration is a terribly painful way to die. It would have been more humane if we had just given her a lethal injection."

Do you see where we are headed? Do you realize that the floodgates have been opened, and death is rushing in to drown anyone who gets in the way of someone's "right" to happiness?

In the 1994 November elections, the state of Oregon said yes to Measure 16, legalizing the killing of terminally ill patients. The law allows doctors to prescribe death drugs to any person who has no more than six months to live. Although there are provisions limiting who and when such suicides could take place, it is obviously a step in the wrong direction.

Television ads promoting Oregon's so-called "Death with Dignity Act" featured a mother who had helped her cancer-stricken, 25-year-old daughter end her suffering. Although the mother said the young woman slipped away "peacefully," an investigation proved otherwise, finding that it took more than 10 hours for death to come.

Dr. Land explains:

Make no mistake about it. America is becoming an increasingly, dangerous place to live — unless you happen to be young, healthy, and productive. And we are quickly, rapidly on a slide into an abyss as dark and as barbarous as anything that happened under the worst excesses of Nazi Germany. Don't think it can't happen here. When it happened in Germany, Germany was the most educated, most literate, most scientifically and educationally advanced country in the world.

Today, in another highly educated country, the Netherlands, "elderly and disabled patients have come to fear" going to the hospital, Mona Charen reports. Why? Because "significant numbers of patients are involuntarily euthanized in Dutch hospitals. We would call it murder."

One thing humanists will never understand is that no amount of education can ever change the human heart. "The heart is deceitful above all things, and desperately wicked" (Jer. 17:9).

The Cold, Clammy Fingers of Death

Dr. Richard Land makes it clear that there is a terrible evil loose in our society — a denial of the sanctity of human life. From the moment abortion was made legal in America, he says, it was inevitable that we could not "confine death to the womb. Its cold clammy fingers would escape into the nursery, and then into the nursing home, and then into the intensive care unit."

Maybe you think because you are a healthy adult you are protected. Maybe so, for a while.

Dr. Land notes that in America today there are 3.2 people working for every one person on Social Security and Medicare. By the time the baby boomers begin to retire, the figures will be down to a little over two to one. By the time the second half of the baby boomer generation begins to retire, only 1.5 people will be working for every one receiving Social Security and Medicare.

These statistics cause us to ask two questions:

First: What has brought about this limited number of our working population? Death. A generation of potential workers will have been murdered by abortionists.

Second: What will happen to all the older baby

boomers who will be thrown into an already over-burdened health care system? The answer is the same — death.

Dr. Land notes that there is a direct correlation between the figures concerning the aging baby boom population and impending health care reforms:

> There's a direct connection between abortion and Dr. Kavorkian's assisted suicide machine. We're getting ready to see a lot of our old and infirm people begin to die before their natural time. And when it happens to the baby boomers, won't it be ironic that they will be allowed to die before their natural time because their children and their grandchildren consider them to be too expensive, too embarrassing, too ill, or too inconvenient? It will be the same pagan, moral rubric that was used to abort our babies. And when that happens, we shouldn't be surprised because the apostle Paul has told us, "Be not deceived, God is not mocked; whatever you sow that shall you reap."

We are about to reap the whirlwind, says Dr. Land, unless we as believers in the Lord Jesus Christ stand up and say, "No more. No more."

We must take a stand for the sacredness of every human being — whether they are old or young, crippled or whole, mentally retarded or intellectually superior. If we don't, says Dr. Land, "there will be no moral difference between the United States of America and those primitive pagan cultures that take their old people out and leave them on ice flows to die of exposure or abandon them in the jungle to die by wild beasts."

When Good People Do Nothing

Our nation is on the verge of moral collapse. Why? Francis Schaeffer answers:

> Not because of the humanist conspiracy but because the Bible-believing Christians in the last 40 years — who have said they know the infinite, personal God — have done nothing. Christians in this country have simply been silent. In fact, much of the evangelical leadership has not raised a voice.

Thousands of babies are murdered in excruciatingly painful abortions every day, but Christian leaders do not object. They do not protest "too much" for fear of alienating their congregations. They do not call for civil disobedience for fear of losing the tax-exempt status for their church.

A similar situation existed in Nazi Germany during World War II as innocent Jews were executed by the millions while the church folded its arms in apathy. Because the German people were led by their political and religious leaders to turn their back on God, life became cheap. Like unborn babies in America today, the Jews were expendable in order to maintain the status quo of society.

Romans 1 tells us "they worshipped and served the creature rather than the Creator." When you worship yourself, then only your life counts. Everyone else is expendable — whether it be the baby in your womb or the parent in the nursing home.

The only hope for our nation is a reasserting of the foundational value upon which this nation was based — the sanctity of every individual human life.

Imposing Morality?

As Christians we are often asked, "What gives you the right to impose your morality on somebody else?"

The answer is simple. Laws against murder, theft, rape, and racism are the legislation of morality. If we don't legislate morality, the immoral will impose their immorality on us.

Dr. Land explains it this way:

> When we pass laws making murder, theft, rape, and racism illegal, we are not so much trying to impose our morality on murderers, thieves, rapists, and racists as we are trying to keep them from imposing their immorality on us and on their victims. When we seek to pass laws restricting a woman's supposed right to kill her unborn baby, we are not so much trying to impose our morality on her as we are on trying to keep her from imposing her immorality on her unborn child.

When Abraham Lincoln ran for president in 1860, people said, "You can't talk about slavery in politics. It's too explosive; it will divide us."

Even people who were opposed to slavery said, "Well, now, I'm personally opposed to slavery, but who am I to impose my morality on slave owners?"

Weren't the slave owners imposing their *immorality* on slaves?

In a speech as the Republican nominee for president in the 1860 presidential campaign, Lincoln said:

> I'm attacked for bringing slavery into the campaign and for my opposition to slavery. I'm told I shouldn't talk about slavery

> in the free states because it isn't there. I
> shouldn't speak about slavery in slaves
> states because it *is* there. I shouldn't speak
> about slavery in politics because that's
> bringing religion into politics. And I
> shouldn't be speaking about slavery from
> the pulpit because that brings politics into
> religion. And there's no single place where
> I can call this wrong thing, wrong.

Sound familiar? If politicians make abortion a campaign issue, they are told it will divide the party. Pastors are told not to preach about abortion from the pulpit because it is a political issue that doesn't concern the church. Pro-life Christians are told by "pro-choice" feminists to "keep your narrow-minded opinions out of my bedroom."

Dr. Land, however, says "we, as a society, have a right and a responsibility to decide that some things are right and some things are wrong and that we're going to make the wrong things illegal."

> We're not going to let the Ku Klux Klan
> impose their insanity on people of color.
> And we have the same right and the same
> responsibility to say that we're not going to
> let people continue to slaughter unborn
> babies. Even if we can't win, we can have
> the right to be faithful. But I believe that we
> can win if we have the courage of our
> convictions and the faith to follow in obe-
> dience the command of our Lord and Sav-
> iour Jesus Christ.

Francis Schaeffer wrote, "Except for the things that the Bible says are specifically sinful, all of life is equally spiritual and that includes, as our forefathers did, standing for the things of freedom and of human life."

The sanctity of life is the defining moral and spiritual issue of our time. Why? Because the consequences affect you, your children, your grandchildren, and will determine the kind of society in which we are going to live.

"Will it be a civilized one or a barbarous one? Will it be a Christian one? Or will it be a pagan one?" Dr. Land asks.

Only you can determine the outcome.

10

Welcome to Sodom and Gomorrah

*'Twas guilt that taught my heart to fear,
And pride my fears relieved;
How precious did that pride appear,
The hour I first believed!*
— Revised lyrics to "Amazing Grace" as
sung at San Francisco's (gay) Glide
Memorial United Methodist
Church

*Sex wasn't made to be "safe." Or
"negotiated." Or "fatal."* — From the
play, "Jeffrey," by Paul Rudnick

Like a cancer eating away at the heart of our nation, abortion demeans life, rendering its people prone to child abuse, elderly abuse, and a horde of other crimes against those too weak to defend themselves. And we are paying a terrible price for those crimes.

As Charles Colson observed, "Politicians justify the taking of innocent life in sterile clinics, and we are terrified by the disregard of life in blood-soaked streets."

A vile stench equal to that of abortion now reaches up to the nostrils of God. A corruption so foul that, if not checked, it will contaminate our entire society.

"The apostle Paul," Baptist pastor David Jeremiah declared, "viewed homosexuality as the cultural culmination of rebellion against God." This practice, which brought down the Roman Empire and other nations, now threatens our own.

Paul, the great Christian theologian who was also a Roman citizen, wrote in the first century A.D. about man's progression into perversion:

> Professing to be wise, they became fools, and changed the glory of the incorruptible God into an image made like corruptible man — and birds and four-footed beasts and creeping things. Therefore God also gave them up to uncleanness, in the lusts of their hearts, to dishonor their bodies among themselves, who exchanged the truth of God for the lie and worshipped and served the creature rather than the Creator who is blessed forever. Amen.
>
> For this reason God gave them up to vile passions, for even their women exchanged the natural use for what is against nature. Likewise, also the men, leaving the natural use of the woman, burned in their lust for one another, men with men committing what is shameful, and receiving in themselves the penalty of their error which was due (Rom. 1:22-27).

During a recent talk show, I listened to a homosexual priest defend and celebrate his lifestyle, which he has recounted in a new book, *Freedom, Absolute Freedom.*

The absurdity of his comments brought to mind the words of a first century fisherman, writing under the inspiration of the Holy Spirit:

> While they promise them liberty, they themselves are slaves of corruption; for by whom a person is overcome, by him also he is brought into bondage (2 Pet. 2:19).

A nation held in the vice of sexual perversion displays a total degeneracy — the sin that caused God in His wrath to "give up the nations."

Thirty-five years ago, I read a book on prophecy by Fuller Seminary professor Wilbur M. Smith, who said, "Homosexuality is like a mist drifting in from the sea." He was right. In those days, one hardly even spoke about such things — especially from the pulpit. Today, unfortunately, the mist has become a torrential downpour that threatens to wash away the very foundations of our nation.

F. LaGard Smith in his book, *Sodom's Second Coming,* writes:

> Centuries ago Sodom and Gomorrah represented a culture not unlike our own in which homosexual perversion became the very symbol of a people who had given up on God and godliness. Nothing pictured more graphically the moral depths to which a society could sink; and God sent down fire from Heaven.

The Bible confirms that the last evil to overtake a society — before it goes over the edge — is an abandonment to lust.

Why It's Called "Sodomy"

The word "gay," says F. LaGard Smith, "applied to

homosexuality is a masterpiece of marketing. The word contains just the right flavor of liberated, happy-go-lucky, debonair rejection of all that is seen by its users as outmoded, restricted, stayed, and circumscribed morality."

One of the myths that Americans are being asked to believe about homosexuals, says Smith, is that they are "cheerful, productive, poetic victims of unjust persecution." Hollywood is aiding this false perception by portraying gays in movie roles as misunderstood, persecuted people who — aside from their "sexual preference" — are really just like you and me.

Are gays really just like you and me?

Not according to Dr. Paul Cameron. He says, "Our surveys show that the average homosexual has around a hundred sex partners in a lifetime. Now some have thousands, but the average is around 100."

Stephen L. Jones, writing in the July 19, 1993, issue of *Christianity Today,* provides even more startling statistics from the famous Bell and Weinberg study. It suggests that about a third of gays have had up to a *thousand* sexual partners in their lifetimes.

Even the most adulterous "heterosexual" would have trouble coming up to that number, but 100 to 1,000 is "normal" for the average homosexual.

"Very few gays are in committed long-term relationships," writes Jones, and "those who are in stable relationships do not tend to be socially monogamous."

Jones quotes from authors McWhirter and Mattison, a gay couple themselves, who write that "to be gay is to be non-monogamous, and that monogamy is an unnatural state" for homosexuals. Why is that? Jones explains that "the homosexual community cannot embrace monogamy because homosexual sex can never produce what God made for sex."

As a result, such sexual activity inevitably leads to perversion.

Is homosexuality just a "sexual preference" to be engaged in by loving, consenting partners? Not according to the facts.

The *Washington Times* reported that, of the homosexuals the U.S. Army had court-martialed for sexual misconduct in the past 4 years, 8 out of every 10 had engaged in sexual assaults against their victims. Of these 102 assault cases, nearly half involved the molestation of children.

Consider Jeffrey Dahmer, who was recently murdered in prison by another inmate. Even convicts consider sexual crimes against children to be deplorable.

You may not consider Dahmer a homosexual since media reports try to downplay his "sexual preference" so as not to give gays a bad name. And no wonder. Dahmer wasn't concerned about the "consent" of his partners as he lured young men to his apartment, drugged them, raped them, killed them, and then ate their body parts.

Few people realize that the Dahmer case was not an isolated occurrence of homosexual behavior. Dr. Paul Cameron, who writes the *Family Research Report,* notes that "the top six U.S. male serial killers were all homosexuals."

Dennis Wheeler, writing in the October 19, 1993, issue of *World News Digest,* compiled these shocking facts:

> John Wayne Gacy raped and killed 33 boys in Chicago. Patrick Kearney murdered 32 young men, cutting them into small pieces after sex and leaving the bodies in trash bags along L.A. freeways. Juan Corona, the migrant worker in California who was

convicted of murdering 25 migrant workers testified at the trial that he had "made love with the corpses."

Even those homosexuals who don't make a *career* of mutilating their "lovers" are known for an astounding degree of savagery when they become violent. Among law enforcement officials, homosexuals are infamous for the overwhelming violence they employ against each other when they discover their partners have been unfaithful or want a separation.

Is this kind of violent, sexual behavior only characteristic of twentieth century homosexuals? Not according to the Bible.

This account of Genesis 19:1-14 from *The Living Bible* provides the reason we call homosexual perversion "sodomy."

That evening the two angels came to the entrance of the city of Sodom, and Lot was sitting there as they arrived. When he saw them, he stood up to meet them and welcomed them.

"Sirs," he said, "come to my home as my guests for the night; you can get up as early as you like and be on your way again."

"Oh, no thanks," they said, "we'll just stretch out here along the street."

But he was very urgent until at last they went home with him, and he set a great feast before them, complete with freshly baked unleavened bread. After the meal, as they were preparing to retire for the night, the men of the city — yes, Sodomites, young and old from all over the city — surrounded the house and shouted to Lot, "Bring out those men to us so we can rape them."

Lot stepped outside to talk to them, shutting the door behind him. "Please, fellows," he begged, "don't do such a wicked thing. Look — I have two virgin daughters, and I'll surrender them to you to do with as you wish. But leave these men alone, for they are under my protection."

"Stand back," they yelled, "who do you think you are? We let this fellow settle among us, and now he tries to tell us what to do! We'll deal with you far worse than with those other men." And they lunged at Lot and began breaking down the door.

But, the two men reached out and pulled Lot in and bolted the door and temporarily blinded the men of Sodom so that they couldn't find the door.

"What relatives do you have here in this city?" the men asked. "Get them out of this place, sons-in-law, sons, daughters, or anyone else; for we will destroy the city completely. The stench of the place has reached to Heaven and God has sent us to destroy it."

Sodom had become a city of homosexuals and bi- sexuals who were not the least bit interested in "sexual relations between consenting adults." Aggressive and forceful in their erotic pursuits, they demanded their "rights." When Lot refused, these "gays" threatened to do worse to Lot than to their intended victims.

The demons of lust may have changed their appearance, but their crude, barbaric behavior remains the same.

Who Are the Homosexuals?

Due to media propaganda, more and more Americans are concluding that the rights of homosexuals are being violated and that they need laws to protect them. Is this true?

Homosexuals are not an oppressed minority. They are better educated than the general population, have higher than average incomes, and exercise extensive political clout. Those are hardly traits of an oppressed minority.

What they don't want us to believe, however, is how much of a minority they really are. Part of the gay rights agenda is to make us think there are millions of them. If they can convince America that "everybody is doing it," then we will begin to think it's not all that bad.

They like to project that 10 percent of our population is gay and lesbian. A recent study, however, concluded that the true figure is *maybe* one or two percent.

No matter. Homosexual activists will continue to distort the truth in an effort to make this decade "the Gay Nineties." They believe that future generations will look back on the 1990s just as blacks now look back on the civil rights movement of the 1960s.

Dennis A. Wheeler confirms this point and notes that the homosexual lobby is working to use the Civil Rights Act to gain for themselves "protected minority status." But they want even more than that. "They want to stifle all resistance to their foul deeds by making opposition to them illegal," writes Wheeler.

Friends in High Places

In June 1994 the *New York Times* reported that

Attorney General Janet Reno "issued an order that would allow homosexuals from other countries to seek political asylum in the United States if they could prove that they were victims of government persecution, solely because of their sexual preference."

Representative Barney Frank, Democrat of Massachusetts, a self-avowed homosexual, praised Ms. Reno's decision and said, "This move by the administration . . . allows gays and lesbians to argue that they can be considered a member of a particular social group which is targeted by their government for persecution."

With such friends in high places, it may be just a matter of time before legislation will force Americans to treat homosexuals with special rights. When that happens, look out! The floodgates will open, and anyone with the courage to challenge these "rights" will become the object of abuse and persecution.

When President Clinton nominated Roberta Achtenberg, an avowed lesbian, for a post in the Department of Housing and Urban Development, she was accompanied to Capitol Hill by her "lesbian lover."

Senator Jesse Helms, in an effort to express his outrage, said, "We are crossing the threshold for the first time in the history of America that a homosexual, a lesbian, has been nominated by a president of the United States for a top job in the U.S. government".

According to Dennis Wheeler, Helms was barraged with criticism from his colleagues. Senator Carol Moseley-Braun protested, "I am frightened to hear the politics of fear and divisiveness and of hatred rear its ugly head on this floor."

Wheeler notes that the hypocrisy of the homosexuals is evident in this case. "While demanding their own freedom of expression," he says, "they have no intention of extending this privilege to their opponents."

They accuse Christians of hatred but make no bones about their violent disgust of those who speak out against the homosexual "lifestyle."

Proud to Be Gay

"Gay Pride Day," which is "celebrated" in cities throughout the United States, has become an opportunity for the "homosexual community" to express their "pride" in their perversions. The news media, of course, is careful not to show us the lewd and crude antics that take place in the middle of public streets during these "parades." Why? Because they don't want American citizens to realize the depravity to which many gays have stooped.

In his book, *The Sexual Dead End*, Stephen Green notes that the homosexual "movement" started in June 1969 in New York City's Greenwich Village, when a riot ensued after police began arresting men involved in perverted acts at the Stonewall Gay Bar.

Militant "gays" then adopted the same language as black civil rights workers and invented "homosexual rights," signaling their declaration of sexual independence and establishing "themselves as a nation within a nation," says Green.

This new identity required new labels. Roy Burns, quoted in Green's book, reveals the homosexual strategy:

> The theme "Proud to be Gay" . . . transferred the stigma from the individual homosexuality to the bigoted opposition. This was a brilliant strategy. Homosexuals were not now sick or perverted. What was sick was the prejudice existing within society against homosexuals and homosexuality. If one was not sick or perverted, then one could be proud to be gay.

You can be sure that anything that happens regarding homosexual rights is no accident. F. LaGard Smith, in *Sodom's Second Coming,* writes: "There is a gay rights network in which many minds are working overtime to advance the goals of the gay rights movement."

The 1972 gay rights platform drawn up by National Coalition of Gay Organizations sets forth the coalition's goals. As you read these objectives provided by Smith, it becomes obvious that their goal is to make it easier for them to prey on young boys:

> Repeal of all laws prohibiting private sexual acts involving consenting adults.
>
> Repeal of all laws prohibiting prostitution, both male and female.
>
> Repeal of all laws governing the age of sexual consent.
>
> Repeal of all legislative provisions that restrict the sex or number of persons entering into a marriage unit, and the extension of legal benefits to all persons who cohabit regardless of sex or numbers.
>
> Enactment of legislation so that child custody, adoption, visitation rights, foster parenting, and the like shall not be denied because of sexual orientation or marital status.
>
> Encouragement and support for sex education courses, prepared and taught by gay women and men, presenting homosexuality as a valid, healthy preference and lifestyle, as a viable alternative to heterosexuality.

It is frightening to see how many of these goals have been or are in the process of being accomplished.

Another product of militant gays is the Twelve Step Gay Agenda, which outlines, in no uncertain terms, the ways they plan to manipulate the media and America in general to bow to their demands. LaGard Smith, in *Sodom's Second Coming,* quotes their blatant strategy:

1. Boldly claim freedom from social restraint and demand independence from the moral order.

2. Associate homosexuals with others in order to achieve legitimacy.

3. Depict decent folks with traditional family values to be the bad guys.

4. Promote the proven lie that gays constitute 10 percent of the population, so there is legitimacy through sheer numbers.

5. Confuse the terminology so that no one realizes the difference between sexual orientation and sexual behavior.

6. Enlist science and medicine in a bogus search for some genetic cause for homosexual behavior.

7. Don't let anyone know what it is that gays actually do sexually.

8. Find creative ways to sidestep what the Bible teaches about homosexual conduct.

9. Open the door to the church and get its blessing for homosexual expression.

10. Break down legal restrictions against sodomy and instead establish legal restrictions against discrimination.

11. Dismantle the American family and make it possible for gays to marry and adopt children.

12. Perpetuate the myths about heterosexual AIDS so that the disease becomes a political asset for the gay movement.

Why are homosexuals so intent on pushing their agenda? Columnist Linda Chavez provides the answer: "Most homosexual activists are not content simply to be left alone or to be accorded only individual rights. Instead, they crave affirmation."

Since their most outspoken opponents are people with religious convictions, homosexuals seek to coerce us into accepting homosexuality as morally equal to heterosexuality. Senator John Kerry has said that this issue will require a lot of education and effort focused at "bringing people along." In other words, Christians need to be "reeducated" into accepting the homosexual lifestyle as a "valid moral choice."

What's wrong with that? Cal Thomas, in a recent column, provides the answer:

> The open celebration of homosexuality represents the final disconnection from a personal God. If the barrier against societal acceptance of homosexuality falls, there will be no other that can stand. . . . When a nation loses its power to resist immorality, it is headed for serious trouble.

Easy Prey

Stephen Green, in his book *The Sexual Dead-End*, includes a chapter titled, "Deceiving the Young." Homosexuals want more access to children because they are easy prey. In fact, young boys and girls are the homosexuals' main target. Why? Because children are unaware of the filthy sexual perversions in which homosexuals engage.

Green explains that "if a potential recruit, a young man or young woman, knew in advance the progressive nature of homosexual activity into more and more degrading activities and if they were aware of exactly what they would end up doing, they might choose to stay well away."

This is exactly why part of the gay agenda is to promote a positive image of the gay and lesbian lifestyle in the public schools. Their goal is to break down any moral barriers that children may have toward these filthy practices, thus making them more willing participants.

Green tells how this happens:

> Research certainly shows that greater involvement in more and more degrading activity correlates with the length of time of homosexual activity. It is, therefore, most important for recruiters to keep the dark side very quiet and to play up the debonair "gay" side as much as possible. A young boy will not respond positively if asked outright to do certain things . . . he has to be progressively initiated.

Make no mistake about it. They want America's children. After all, with the AIDS epidemic and their inability to reproduce, gays have to find some way to populate their ranks. There are two ways to do that: By recruiting young boys and girls into the homosexual lifestyle and by adopting them into their homes.

God's Outcry Against It

What does the Bible say about homosexuality?
Genesis 18 records the words God spoke to Abraham:

> The Lord said, "Because the outcry against

Sodom and Gomorrah is great, and because their sin is very grievous, I will go
down now and see whether they have done
altogether according to the outcry against
it that has come to Me; and if not, I will
know" (Gen. 18:20-21).

Something was so foul about the activities going on
in Sodom and Gomorrah that creation itself cried out
against it. It was the outcry of the land.

God spoke clearly in His Word: "You shall not lie
with a male as with a woman. It is an abomination" (Lev.
18:22). The word abomination means something that is
loathsome, abhorrent, detestable.

The consequences of breaking God's command meant
death: "If a man lies with a male as he lies with a woman,
both of them have committed an abomination. They will
surely be put to death, their blood shall be upon them"
(Lev. 20:13).

Remember, this is Old Testament law. As Christians,
we are under the New Covenant, and the death penalty is
not employed today against those who commit homosexual acts or any other kind of sexual sin.

That does not alleviate our responsibility to confront
homosexuals with their sin.

Like Jesus, we must speak the truth in love. When
confronting the hypocritical Pharisees, He did so out of
love. Jesus wanted them to realize that their hearts were
not right with God. Many of the religious leaders were
offended by the truth He spoke, while others embraced the
gospel.

Stephen L. Jones, writing in *Christianity Today,* puts
it this way:

Christ is our perfect model of love and
compassion, and we have much to learn

from his love for sinners and participation in their lives. But, he did not just ooze warm fuzzies. Christ also had the gall to tell others how to live their lives, to insist that His truth was the only truth, and to claim that He alone was the way to God. In short, Jesus was what many people today would call a narrow-minded bigot.

When we, as Christ's church, proclaim the message we have received from Him, we risk being called old-fashioned and narrow-minded. "We must face the reality that Christianity 'discriminates,'" says Jones, because "it says one path is the right way."

Let us also remember that the one right way is also the only way to freedom for our homosexual friends trapped in their compulsive and destructive perversion.

F. LaGard Smith in *Sodom's Second Coming* writes that we need to differentiate between "those who have been tempted, those who have stumbled and fallen and who have had a homosexual experience, and the militant gays."

Stephen Jones notes that few people today choose to have homosexual inclinations. He says genetic factors "may give some a push in the direction of homosexual preference." In addition, "disordered family relationships" leave people confused about their sexual identity as does "early homosexual experiences of seduction or abuse."

Jack Hayford notes that loneliness draws many into homosexuality: "They trade off their body for acceptance." Hayford also points out that to be tempted and even to succumb to a temptation in no way makes one a homosexual. "We are all capable of sin," Hayford says.

Homosexuality is no worse than any other sin as

First Corinthian 6:9-11 makes clear:

> ... Do not be deceived, neither fornicators
> nor idolaters, nor adulterers, nor homo-
> sexuals, nor sodomites, nor thieves, nor
> covetous, nor drunkards, nor revilers, nor
> extortioners will inherit the Kingdom of
> God. And such were some of you. But you
> were washed, but you were sanctified, but
> you were justified in the name of the Lord
> Jesus and by the Spirit of our God.

Healing and forgiveness are available to all who confess their sins and acknowledge the sanctifying blood of Jesus as their only hope.

Once Gay Always Gay?

Some homosexuals balk at the idea that they can be changed and that healing is available. Why does this infuriate them? Because they don't want to change!

Others, however, want to be free from their sinful lifestyle, but have been led to believe that there is no way out. They have believed the lie that they were born that way and "once gay always gay."

Joseph Nicolois, author of *Reparative Therapy of Male Homosexuality,* condemns modern psychology and psychiatry that has "abandoned a whole population of people who feel dissatisfied with homosexuality."

A few medical professionals have been courageous enough to contradict "politically correct" wisdom. Stephen Green in his book, *Sexual Dead-End*, notes that "indi-vidual psychoanalysts continue to regard homosexuality as pathological and treatable."

One of those is Charles Socarides, a professor at the Albert Einstein College of Medicine and a leading expert on homosexuality, who debunks the idea that homosexuality is "inborn." Writing in the *Journal of Psychiatry*, he concludes:

> Homosexuality, the choice of a partner of the same sex for orgiastic satisfaction is not innate. There is no connection between sexual instinct and the choice of sexual object; such an object choice is learned, acquired behavior. There is no inevitable, genetically inborn propensity towards the choice of a partner of either the same or opposite sex.

Same-sex behavior is not natural, and most homosexuals know it. The first homosexual experience usually results from an older person preying on a defenseless child. Many who were drawn into such perverted sex have written about the disgust that accompanied their first homosexual experience.

Let's face it — homosexual sex is nothing less than moral corruption and degradation.

F. LaGard Smith, in his book, *Sodom's Second Coming*, describes the acts in which homosexuals engage, which he calls "the dark side of being gay." These practices are so foul that God himself says if we continue to tolerate them, punishment is certain: "For the land is defiled; therefore I will visit the punishment of its iniquity upon it, and the land vomits out its inhabitants" (Lev. 18:25).

Those who participate in these vile acts know what they are doing is wrong. Their own conscience condemns them, and "they are without excuse" (Rom. 1:20). Even most primitive cultures throughout history have not tolerated homosexual behavior because it goes against every natural instinct within mankind.

Those who practice this kind of sin experience fear

and guilt — not because society makes them feel guilty but because they are guilty of breaking the law God has put in their heart.

They must either deal with God's Word as it stands or find some method of explaining it away. Even if they find some theological loophole, their consciences will not let them escape the guilt. They *know* what they are doing is wrong. Many, who can't live with the pain, commit suicide, which is at epidemic proportions within the homosexual community.

To add to their discontent is the constant threat of the deadly, sexually transmitted disease — AIDS.

What's So Gay About AIDS?

An article in the *Christian Century* noted that of those who have died as a result of AIDS in San Francisco, "Ninety-seven percent of the individuals who have contracted AIDS have been homosexual or bisexual men."

In his book, *Right from the Beginning,* Patrick J. Buchanan explains the reason for the spread of AIDS among homosexuals:

> Promiscuous sodomy — unnatural, un-sanitary sexual relations between males, which every great religion teaches is im-moral — is the cause of AIDS. Anal sex between consenting adults is spreading the virus from one homosexual to another, thence into the needles of addicts and the blood supply of hemophiliacs.

Make no mistake about it: The homosexual agenda threatens our children, our families, and the physical and moral health of our society. No nation in history that has tolerated such behavior has survived.

We must stop the propaganda machine and resist the

appeal for "tolerance." And we must resist the attempt of homosexuals and the media to label anyone opposed to that lifestyle as "homophobic."

Buchanan writes that name-calling has replaced common sense when dealing with the AIDS issue and any practical methods of containing the spread of the disease:

> Several years ago when I wrote that New York City, on the eve of that celebration of sodomy known as "Gay Pride Week," should shut down the squalid little "love nests" called bathhouses, the incubators of the disease, I was denounced as a "homophobe" by the governor and mayor of New York. Because these men were morally confused, men and boys continued infecting one another in the bathhouses and continued killing one another.

Why does the homosexual community refuse to accept responsibility for the AIDS epidemic? Because to do so would mean they must alter their lifestyle. Instead, they demand a cure — no matter what the cost.

A *USA Today* editorial noted that "the AIDS lobby of gays and lesbians has antagonized nearly every other medical special interest organization seeking funds for cancer and heart research and other worthy causes. The lobby is so strong, especially with basketball star Magic Johnson's admitting to being HIV positive, that we are told it can happen to anyone."

That is the lie they want us to believe, but the truth is that the AIDS problem results from behavior that can be altered but isn't. Still, the myth is propagated, and even President Clinton bought into the lie.

During the presidential campaign of 1992, Bill Clinton, according to a May 20,1992, *USA Today* report, "vowed to push AIDS education to give 'our children the hard truth and a chance to save their lives.'"

Speaking to 500 people from various gay groups, Clinton said, "If I could wave my arm for those of you who are HIV positive and make it go away tomorrow, I would do it — so help me God, I would."

An effective remedy would be to enforce the sodomy laws that are still on the books in many states and pass federal legislation making unhealthy, unnatural sexual acts illegal. Instead of dealing with promiscuous gays who are carrying and spreading the disease, the president and the surgeon general of the United States opted for a bandaid type treatment — condom education for elementary students.

Patrick Buchanan explains why this is a ludicrous policy:

> Today nine year olds are being educated in the use of condoms. But it is not nine year olds who are buggering one another with abandon, spreading this deadly virus. It is not nine year olds who threaten doctors, dentists, health workers, hemophiliacs, and the rest of society by their refusal to curb their ludicrous appetites by which the militant homosexuals are killing themselves. What precisely is "gay" about that?

Government officials need to turn their attention to those who are already infected and implement a rational, medical response that would treat AIDS as any other communicable disease. This is the most compassionate approach both for homosexuals and the rest of us.

Let Gays Be Gay?

Should Christians back off and let gays be gay?

Alexander F. C. Webster, Orthodox priest and research fellow at the Ethics and Public Policy Center of the Virginia Army National Guard, says, No! In an article titled, "Homosexuals in Uniform," in the February 8, 1993, issue of *Christianity Today,* Chaplain Webster writes:

> Let's be clear about what is and what is not at stake in this controversy. Homosexual practice is wrong, and it is not homophobic to say so. No faithful Christian or any advocate of virtue should acquiesce on this issue just because discussion of it is couched in the twisted terminology of "gay rights."
> ... A public rejection of demands to protect homosexual behavior ... must be based on an affirmation of the traditional virtues associated with chastity, matrimonial love, and genuine compassion for others. Loving the homosexual as a person does not preclude our being truthful about homosexual behavior."

So what is the truth about homosexual behavior? Why is it so abominable to God?

To answer that question, we must first ask: What is it that homosexuals *do*? I will leave you to research that answer in other books, like F. LaGard Smith's *Sodom's Second Coming,* published by Harvest House, and *The Sexual Dead-End* by Stephen Green (Broadview Books, P.O. Box 782, London, S.W. 162YT England).

Suffice it to say, in the words of Chaplain Webster: "The present issue is not safe verses unsafe sex, but rather decent verses indecent. Sodomy, no matter how it is legitimized, is still a filthy practice at odds with human anatomy."

President Clinton, however, decided that such practices merit the support and endorsement of an executive order when he advocated "tolerance" for practicing homosexuals in the military and society at large. Chaplain Webster says this presidential action "cloaks what amounts to a political *validation* of an unnatural, unhealthy, and ungodly lifestyle."

Many in the military have argued, says Webster, "that homosexuals in uniform will have a debilitating effect on the missions of the armed forces and on the morale of any soldier who has ever taken a shower or slept in close quarters with his buddies."

When a nation passes laws or establishes policies that run counter to the Word of God — not to mention common sense — one need only look up to see the storm clouds of judgment hovering overhead.

What should Christians do? Webster has this advice for us:

> The bottom line for Christians remains the clearly expressed will of God and Holy Scripture. . . . the texts that address homosexuality are plain in their meaning. The chief sin of Sodom was sodomy, not inhospitality, and the Church has always taught this truth; beginning with Jude 7.

What does Jude 7 say? "Sodom and Gomorrah, and the cities around them . . . having given themselves over to sexual immorality and gone after strange flesh, are set forth as an example, suffering the vengeance of eternal fire."

F. LaGard Smith sums up the problem faced by us as Christians living in a secular society:

> What we are witnessing today in the homosexual assault against America's moral

values is nothing short of Sodom's second coming, and we, too, face God's judgment. It's time for a sober assessment, not just of activist homosexuals, but of the Church, our own families, and each one of us individually. Have we like Lot "pitched our tents toward Sodom"?

We must go forth, with an assurance grounded in the Word of God and a deep concern for the moral and spiritual health of our nation — or face God's wrath as did Sodom and Gomorrah.

This is one issue on which we dare not remain silent.

11

Yearning to Breathe Free

For all our alarm, it is clear that the religious right is responding to a real hunger in our society . . . a deep-seated yearning for stable values.
— Norman Lear

When I first traveled overseas many years ago, I was struck by scenes that depicted the cheapness of human life. I saw workmen building sidewalks and high rises using primitive tools and wooden implements. Women worked beside them, carrying stacks of bricks on their heads, climbing up flimsy ladders made of poles tied together with rope.

These images stand out in my mind today in contrast to the dignity that Americans accord even the most common laborer.

Later in my travels, I would encounter at railway stations and on street corners adults and children alike wrapped in rags, living and sleeping under stairwells, hoping for the occasional coin or morsel of food from the hand of a sympathetic traveler. I couldn't help but think that much of the world never sees in a lifetime the quantity of food the American housewife can choose in just one trip to the supermarket.

On such days during my travels, I would grow home-sick and reflect on the proud lady who stands in New York Harbor, holding high the torch of freedom and crying,

> Give me your tired, your poor,
> Your huddled masses yearning to breathe free,
> The wretched refuse of your teaming shore.
> Send these, the homeless, tempest tossed to me.
> I lift my lamp beside the golden door.

In subsequent years, whenever the wheels of my jet touch down in Boston or New York, there are tears and a prayer: "God bless America."

And then I ask: Is this abundance and this freedom ours merely by chance? Is it wholly due to what Americans like to perceive as the result of hard work and ingenuity? If God, indeed, has blessed America, why?

The freedoms we have in the United States, according to Christian statesman, Francis Schaeffer, "are absolutely unique in the world." They are not rooted in the Greek city-states, as modern educators teach. "All you have to do is read Plato's Republic, and you will understand the Greek city-states never had any concept of the freedoms that we have," Schaeffer reminds Americans. "What we have and take so poorly for granted is unique."

A Turning Tide?

If we are to maintain our unique freedoms, we must reverse the trend toward humanism that has swallowed up an entire generation of Americans with its treacherous lies.

"To destroy a country," Solzhenitsyn wrote, "you must first cut its roots."

With that in mind, Patrick Buchanan declares: "If America's roots are in Judeo-Christian values and traditions, they have in large measure been severed." Why is that? Because "religion is at the root of morality, and morality is the basis of law," notes Buchanan.

Other nations have already discovered that religious values are essential for a moral and prosperous society.

Charles Colson, in a column written for *Christianity Today,* makes this observation:

> The irony is exquisite. While formerly "godless Communists," albeit for practical reasons, are looking to religious values to undergird their deteriorating social structures, the ostensibly "Christian West" is doing everything it can to purge itself of those same values.

Ralph Reed, executive director of the Christian Coalition, wrote in the *Wall Street Journal* about Soviet scientists who were visiting in the United States. They told a Washington, DC church congregation, "We have seen that totalitarianism cannot destroy spiritual life. And now as totalitarianism itself is being destroyed, and people move from slavery to freedom, we need a new system of values — spiritual values."

The book, *The Rebirth of America,* published by the DeMoss Foundation, notes that the United States suffers from memory loss:

> God has showered upon America 200 years of blessing as she acknowledged and obeyed her Creator. America has led the world in medical and technical advance-

ment. The nation has pioneered in space, pushed back the frontiers of science, and given its citizens the world's highest standard of living. Unfortunately, we have suffered a fatal lapse of memory.

The 1994 landslide victory by the Republican party indicates that Americans may be recovering from their amnesia. This revolutionary election, in which Americans overwhelmingly cast their votes for conservative senators, representatives, and governors, may indicate a "turning tide" in political policy in our nation.

While we can expect the "new Congress" to make many sweeping changes, we, as Christians, must realize that just because a politician is conservative in his views does not make him a Christian. He may be just as much a humanist as the liberal seated across the Senate chamber aisle.

Francis Schaeffer, speaking in the 1980s, said that "a conservative humanism is no better than a liberal humanism." In other words, any political view — whether liberal or conservative, socialistic or democratic — that values man above God can only produce a humanistic, godless society.

Prayer — Or Politics as Usual?

While the Republican "Contract with America" lists some very courageous and much-needed reforms, I can't help but notice that they neglected to mention the moral issues that we have discussed in this book — the issues that will determine the very future of our nation. In fact, the resolution of these very issues — abortion, homosexuality, and education— will determine whether we continue to exist as a nation at all.

Columnist Samuel Francis, writing on November 20,

1994, made this observation:

> What is most striking about the Contract is
> what isn't in it . . . "cultural issues." Since
> it is precisely these issues that have been
> at the heart of the conservative critique of
> . . . the liberalism that has dominated this
> country for 60 years, there's very little in
> the Contract for real rightists to "moo"
> about. Thus the Contract says nothing
> about abortion or school prayer, the staple
> issues of the religious right that contrib-
> uted significantly to the Republican vic-
> tory. It says nothing about reversing judi-
> cial activism or . . . homosexuals in the
> military or about the matter of "homo-
> sexual rights" in general.

Gary Bauer, head of Family Research Council, comments that the November 1994 elections reflected the
voters "aversion to big government and high taxes" and "a
grave concern about moral decline."

One poll taken after the election indicated that 56
percent of Americans believe the country's problems are
"primarily moral and cultural in nature."

When a constitutional amendment regarding prayer
in public schools was suggested by the new Republican
leadership, several leaders of church denominations immediately denounced the call for the amendment. Why?
They didn't want the government dictating a specific
prayer for Christian children to pray. To get around the
problem, some politicians are now suggesting a "moment
of silence" in the classroom.

In his November 20, 1994, editorial, columnist Cal
Thomas, in quoting theologian Carl Henry, explains why
such a procedure would be a hoax:

Silent awe in the presence of the universe
may be a humanist definition of prayer, but
Christianity is a religion of verbal communication between man and God, a religion
of divine verbal revelation. Christianity
should not be further discriminated against
by smuggling in a pseudo-option.

As far as I'm concerned, the call for prayer in our
schools must be a heart-felt desire to honor and acknowledge the God of the Bible. If not, it will only be a pharisaic
attempt to reform America with a small dose of religion
and an effort to placate conservative Christians, in hopes
we will forget about the thousands of babies being legally
slaughtered in America every day.

Prayer in our public schools is certainly in order, but
it alone will not reverse more than 40 years of entrenched
humanism fostered by the National Education Association. Besides, the problems that plague America's school
corridors are simply representative of American society at
large.

The violence and crime and immorality perpetrated
on the streets finds its way into the hallways of America's
schools. The lack of integrity, moral values, and humanistic ideas stimulated by a godless culture are rampant in
our educational institutions, where such philosophies are
not only bred but fostered.

Former Surgeon General Jocelyn Elders, who repre-
sents the secular mindset and who advocated giving
condoms to elementary students, was asked by an inter-
viewer: "What should we be doing about crime and
violence?"

"I don't know," she replied. "I do feel strongly we
need to take the tools of violence out of the hands of
children. I definitely support the five-day waiting period

for buying handguns. We should ban automatic assault weapons. We should stop giving our children toy guns."

Something's wrong when the nation's highest ranking medical doctor wants to give condoms to fifth graders, favors allowing homosexuals in the Boy Scouts, and thinks taking toy guns out of the hands of children will end the violence in America. It seems the secularists always are willing to place restrictions on anything except sex.

America's Moral Decline

Some react with indifference. "So what?" they ask. So what if the surgeon general wants to give condoms to elementary students?"

Peter Marshall in *The Light and the Glory,* notes this attitude is at the heart of our problem:

> The most significant index of the extent of our moral decay is our very indifference to it. Pornography has insinuated itself into practically every level of our daily life, including our language. Corrupt personal and business practices, which once would have erupted into major scandals, today seem scarcely scandalous. Where once we would have been up in arms, speaking out, writing letters, and voting, now we just shake our heads and count it as another sign of the times.

Richard C. Halverson, in his book, *The Timelessness of Jesus Christ,* explains how such indifference to morality has created a hedonistic culture in America:

> An autobiography written some years ago, *My Life and Loves,* by Frank Harris, contains the author's account of the four hun-

> dred times he seduced women. Giving in
> clear, candid, careful detail his technique
> from the beginning of the seduction to its
> consummation, that book and many more
> like it written by former wives and lovers
> is available on bookstands competing with
> popular magazines and movies explicit in
> the portrayal of the intimacies of sex. This
> is the ultimate in depravity, pandering por-
> nography to a culture which eats it up.

In America today, *Playboy* magazine is treated with
as much respect as *Time* and *Newsweek,* in spite of the fact
that numerous studies link pornography to crimes committed by sex offenders. According to FBI statistics, 81
percent of serial killers, 86 percent of rapists, and 87
percent of those convicted of sex crimes against female
children admitted to regular use of pornography — much
of it hard-core.

In his message, "A Christian Manifesto," Francis
Schaeffer describes the moral decline in our nation over
the last 80 years — a decline that has attributed to sexual
permissiveness, pornography, violence in the public
schools, the breakdown of the family, abortion, infanticide (killing of newborn babies), and increased euthanasia.

Schaeffer, however, saw these as only "isolated bits
and pieces" that are only *"symptoms* of a deeper problem."

What is the real problem? Schaeffer says it is "a
change in our society from a Judeo-Christian conscience
to a humanistic one."

When the Law is God

According to Schaeffer, humanism means that "man

is the measure of all things" and that "material energy shaped by pure chance is the final reality." The natural result of a philosophy that has no place for any knowledge of God, Schaeffer says, will always be humanism — the worship of man. Such thinking leaves a vacuum, however, and gives no meaning to life, provides no value system, and supplies no basis for law.

Why? Because "man has no possible source of knowledge except what man, beginning from himself, can find out by his own observation." As a result, "any value system must come arbitrarily from man himself by arbitrary choice," Schaeffer says.

Any basis of law, then, "becomes arbitrary, as certain people make decisions as to what is best for the good of society at the given moment. This is the real reason for the breakdown in morals in our country," this contemporary American statesman notes.

Thomas Jefferson declared: "God who gave us life gave us liberty. Can the liberties of a nation be secure when we have removed a conviction that these liberties are the gift of God?"

The answer is no. And the result is apparent. Schaeffer explains that this lack of conviction is why our Supreme Court now functions so thoroughly upon the fact of arbitrary law:

> They have no basis for law that is fixed; therefore, like the young person who decides to live heathenistically upon his own arbitrary values, society is now doing the same thing legally. The certain few people come together and decide what they arbitrarily believe is for the good of the society at the given moment, and that becomes law.

This new dominant world view is exactly opposite from that of our founding fathers who established this country on the basis that there is a God, our Creator, who gave us "inalienable rights."

Dr. Richard Land of the Southern Baptist Christian Life Committee notes that "the most important defining document in the history of this country is the Declaration of Independence." In declaring our independence from Great Britain, our forefathers defined our "inalienable rights" as "life, liberty, and the pursuit of happiness."

"If you are a human being," says Land, "you have the right to life. Our forefathers said we are endowed by our Creator with the right to life."

In 1973, however, the United States Supreme Court denied the right to life to a generation of children and gave that right to their mothers and their mothers' doctors. As a result, over 25 million mothers chose death — not life — for their pre-born babies.

What is an inalienable right? Dr. Land provides the answer: "It is a right that can't be taken away. It's a right that cannot be given away. It's a right that can't be granted. It's a right that cannot be sold or bought."

This fact is critical to our freedom. Why?

Schaeffer explains: "If the state gives the rights, it can take them away; they're not inalienable. If the state gives the rights, they can change them and manipulate them."

Isn't that exactly what is happening in America today? Aren't the courts reversing the mandates of voters? Almost every controversial issue passed by state legislatures or by voter referendums has been challenged in the courts, where, in many cases, the will of the people has been thrown out.

Term limits for senators and congressmen, passed by the voters of several states, has been determined "unconstitutional" by the courts.

States that did not want to grant "special rights" to homosexuals have faced boycotts and extensive legal battles that eventually overturned the wishes of the people.

State laws limiting how and when abortions could take place have been held up for years because of numerous court appeals, which have gone all the way to the Supreme Court. Although some, like the "Abortion Control Act" in Pennsylvania, made it through, the laws were weakened in the process, and hundreds of babies died in the interim.

The Cultural War

What is going on in America?

F. LaGard Smith says, "It's not just *Roe v. Wade; Bowers v. Hardwick;* it's right verses wrong, morality verses immorality, good verses evil, civilization verses anarchy."

We are engaged in a cultural war for the hearts and minds of American citizens. Who are the opposing factions in the battle? You may be surprised to learn that the radical left considers *you,* the Bible-believing, born-again Christian and the church you attend, their greatest enemy.

Why? Because, whether we like it or not, we are the "keepers of morality" for our society. And "society not only has the right but the responsibility to impose a collective sense of morality," says Smith.

This brings us back, once again, to the two issues that — more than any others — challenge the level of morality in our nation: abortion and homosexual "rights."

In order to achieve these so-called "rights," the activists in these movements have a common goal: "The deliberate curtailment of the free exercise of religion in America," says Smith. In other words, there is an all-out assault to curtail religious expression and especially Christian involvement in the political arena. Liberal media attacks against the Christian Coalition before and after the 1994 elections are a prime example of the left's desire to silence us.

Why are we focusing on the issue of gay rights? Because giving homosexuals the rights they are demanding means taking away *our* religious rights.

"Make no mistake about it," says Smith, " 'gay rights' means the elevation of the right to have immoral homosexual relations over the right to act pursuant to one's religious conscience." In effect, immorality becomes more important than morality.

Smith explains how this happens:

> It happens when my mother or perhaps yours puts an ad in the paper to rent out her garage apartment. If a couple shows up at her door and discloses that they are gay, my mother could not in good conscience rent to them. But under a typical gay rights statute or ordinance, she would be in violation of law for refusing to do so. Or consider the firm of Christian lawyers who wish to hire only practicing Christians on their staff. Under a typical gay rights statute or ordinance, they would be put in the position of either violating their own consciences by hiring, or violating the law for refusing to hire a legal secretary who was openly homosexual.

Surely religious organizations would be exempt from such statutes, you say. Yes, in some cases, but what about religious *individuals?*

Politicians often assume they need to protect gays against hateful discrimination by Christians. They fail to realize that "it is not hatred from which we operate but conscience," says Smith. "It is not the homosexual we can't live with if we cave into our beliefs, but ourselves."

Our concerns go beyond laws governing renting to or hiring gays. What about the push for gay marriages and the adoption of children by gay couples? What about their attempts to use public education to indoctrinate children in the gay lifestyle? Will we, as Christians, throw up our hands and give up just as the battle lines are being drawn?

We must not. We cannot. "There is no room for compromise, only competition," says LaGard Smith. "Once you square off relative morality against absolute morality, it is a fight to the death. They can't both survive."

The Supreme Battle Ground

Where will the battle for morality and religious freedom be fought? Where it has been fought for years: the Supreme Court of the United States.

In his book, *Right from the Beginning,* Patrick J. Buchanan explains why Christians have been on the losing side of this fight for the past 30 years:

> In a nation whose Declaration of Independence presupposes the existence of a Supreme Being, God, the Bible, and the Ten Commandments have been ordered out of the public schools and for 30 years, one cowardly Congress after another has refused to slap down our legislating justices, and no president has dared stand up to them.

There, in a nutshell, is the problem we face.

Abraham Lincoln, when confronted by the same dilemma, challenged judicial supremacy with these words:

> If the policy of the government upon vital
> questions affecting the whole people is to
> be irrevocably fixed by the decisions of the
> Supreme Court . . . the people will have
> ceased to be their own rulers, having to that
> extent practically resigned their govern-
> ment into the hands of that eminent tribu-
> nal.

That is exactly where we are today. The people of the
United States have ceased to be governed by their elected
officials. Instead, we are now governed by the Supreme
Court, which for 30 years, according to Buchanan "has
been on a rampage over the laws and customs and constitutional mores of the American people."

Having abused their power, these nine justices impose "their own idea of the good society," while the entire
nation must wait "for Mondays in October to learn from
Olympus what kind of state legislatures we may have,
whether the death penalty shall be permissible, whether
abortion is a constitutional right, whether racial quotas are
to be a permanent feature of America's future," writes
Buchanan.

The main fault lies not with the court but with our
elected leaders who do not restrict the federal courts,
including the U.S. Supreme Court. The Founding Fathers
gave that right to our elected representatives and the
residing president.

"How does one break the power of an imperial
judiciary?" asks Buchanan. "How do conservatives who
revere the Constitution reign in a renegade court?"

One way is to elect presidents who will appoint
justices who will uphold moral values. Another way is for
the president to take a public stand against the power of
the nine who reign over America.

When Thomas Jefferson was ordered to turn his presidential papers over and appear in a Richmond Court, he simply refused.

"A strong and self-confident president," writes Buchanan, "should, when the next decision of dubious constitutionality is handed down, send Congress legislation carefully restricting the court's right to decide such matters."

We must face the fact that today, in the United States, our nation is governed by the tyranny of the Supreme Court.

When Tyranny Rules

When we think of tyranny, we think of Mao's China, Stalin's Russia, or Castro's Cuba.

Christian philosopher Francis Schaeffer in a message given some years ago, compared our humanistic American schools to those of Communist Russia. Before the fall of Communism, it was illegal, even criminal, to teach religion to children or even to mention the name of God in Russia's schools. Today, all religious teaching is banned by law in America's public classrooms, making them just as secular as schools once were in Soviet Russia.

Prayer and Bible reading are prohibited and considered "unconstitutional" within the confines of America's school grounds — including the playground and school bus.

Congress opens with prayer. "Why?" asks Schaeffer. "Because Congress has always opened with prayer. Yet, it is illegal for youngsters to meet and pray on the geographical location of the public schools."

Schaeffer describes America's present situation as tyranny. "Tyranny! That's what we face," he says. "We face a world view forced upon us by the courts and the government."

What should we do about this tyranny that seeks to take away our personal and religious freedom?

"We who are Christians and others who love liberty should be acting in our day as the founding fathers acted in their day," says Schaeffer. He then adds:

> Those who founded this country believed they were facing tyranny. All you have to do is read their writings. That's why the [Revolutionary] War was fought. That's why this country was founded. They believed that God never, never, never wanted people to be under tyrannical governments. They did it not as a pragmatic or economical thing, although that was also involved, I guess, but for principle. They were against tyranny.

What would the Pilgrims, the Puritans, or our founding fathers do if they lived today? Would they stand idly by while their religious freedoms were stripped away? No. That is why they left Europe and came to the New World — for religious freedom. That is why men like Thomas Jefferson, Samuel Adams, Patrick Henry, George Washington, and others founded this nation on religious principles — because they wanted to safeguard their religious and personal freedoms.

Our founding fathers were not in favor of a theocracy, and neither should we be. This country was founded on the principle of freedom for everybody, not just Christians. We should, however, be committed to preserving the freedoms for which our forefathers fought and died, pledging, as they did, "our lives, our fortunes, and our sacred honor."

Francis Schaeffer says the responsibility does not rest solely on the shoulders of our Christian leaders, but on us as American citizens. He then asks these pointed questions:

> Where have the Christian lawyers been? Why haven't they been challenging this change in the view of what the First Amendment means? Where have the Christian doctors been in speaking out against the rise of the abortion clinics? Where have the Christian businessmen been, to put their lives and their work on the line concerning these things which they would say as Christians are central to them? Where have the Christian educators been as we have lost our educational system? Where have we been? Where have each of you been? What's happened in the last 40 years?

"When a government commands that which is contrary to the law of God," says Schaeffer, "it abrogates its authority." When that happens, "at a certain point, it is not only the privilege, but it is the duty of the Christian to disobey the government. That's what the founding fathers did. That's what the early Christians did."

With that thought in mind, consider these words of Dr. James Dobson, quoted by Erwin W. Lutzer in his book, *Why Are We the Enemy?*:

> At what point will we be willing to defend what we believe? Will parents object if their children are routinely indoctrinated in homosexual ideology or occultism in the public schools? Will we object if the state tells pastors what they can or can't say from the pulpit? . . . Will we object if the state assumes "ownership" of our children

and tells us how to rear them or else lose custody? Will we object if every church has to hire a homosexual to satisfy a quota obligation?

Lutzer then provides the example of an evangelical pastor in Sweden who preached a sermon on Sodom and Gomorrah. As a result, he was convicted of "verbal violence" against homosexuals and sentenced to a four-week prison term.

When Freedom Costs

Erwin W. Lutzer writes about what happened in 1943, when the church in Germany adopted the Arian clause, which denied the pulpit to ordained ministers of Jewish blood. One pastor, Dietrich Bonhoeffer, protested, saying that the church should "jam the spokes of the wheel of the state if the persecution of the Jews should continue."

Although some clergymen joined in his public protest, most remained silent. What was the result of Bonhoeffer's refusal to obey an immoral law? He was imprisoned by the Nazis and executed.

That could never happen here, you say.

What about Randall Terry who has been imprisoned for months at a time on numerous occasions because he dared to organize opposition and public protest to the abortion industry?

Many Christians do not agree with the methods of Operation Rescue, which promotes peaceful, prayerful blockage of abortion clinics. But I wonder where America would be today if these brave men and women did not continue to take a public stand, disobey the government, and lay their bodies on the line for the babies scheduled to die in abortion "clinics."

Among the positive outcomes is the fact that these rescuers raised the conscience of America by acting on what they believed — that abortion is the murder of innocent babies.

Today the abortion rate is dropping — if even only slightly. Adoptions are on the rise. Abortion clinics are shutting down, and doctors are refusing to perform abortions — some out of fear for their reputations, others out of moral conviction.

The early Christians disobeyed the Roman government, acknowledging that "Christ must be the final Lord, not Caesar and not society," says Schaeffer.

Bonhoeffer's friend, Martin Niemoller, came to the same conclusion and decided not to give up despite the danger. He eventually rallied 6,000 pastors who became the nucleus of the "confessing church."

Niemoller, like his friend, did not escape persecution and was imprisoned by Hitler and later placed in solitary confinement. Although freed after the war, Niemoller never forgot what his early silence had cost him. Whenever he concluded a speech, he ended with these now famous words:

> They came for the Communists, and I didn't object — for I was not a Communist. They came for the socialists, and I didn't object because I was not a socialist. They then came for the labor leaders, and I didn't object because I was not a labor leader. They came for the Jews, and I didn't object because I was not a Jew. Then they came for me, and there was no one left to object.

Who will speak while there is still time in America and some freedoms remain?

Will the church of Jesus Christ have the courage to

take a stand against the evils in our society before they come for us?

Some Christians believe we should stay away from social and political issues and simply confine ourselves to our churches.

Dr. Richard Land asks: "Should we withdraw from the cultural and political arena, and just concentrate on our churches or should we seek to develop a world view through which we can be active and informed citizens?"

Dr. James Dobson provides the answer to that question:

> The bottom line is that believers cannot choose to remain silent under the guise of preaching the gospel. If the liberal social planners continue to have their way, no one will be exempt from their influence. After all, it is our children, our schools, and our right to preach the gospel that is at stake. We cannot retreat.

Queen Esther thought she would be safe if she remained silent in the court of the evil King Ahasuerus even though her own people, the Jews, were about to be murdered. Her uncle Mordecai, however, challenged her to consider the situation:

> "Do not think in your heart that you will escape in the king's palace any more than all the other Jews. For if you remain completely silent at this time, relief and deliverance will arise for the Jews from another place, but you and your father's house will perish. Yet who knows whether you have come to the kingdom for such a time as this?" (Esther 4:13-14).

As a result of Esther's courage to speak up for her people, disaster was averted and her countrymen spared.

The time has come for us to speak up. If we don't, who will?

The Choice

Are you willing to take a stand to protect that which we value most as Christians — life? The choice is yours.

God, speaking through Moses to his people, presented them with this challenge:

> "I have set before you today life and good, death and evil, in that I command you today to love the Lord your God, to walk in His ways, and to keep His commandments, His statues, and His judgments, that you may live and multiply; and the Lord your God will bless you in the land which you go to possess. But if your heart turns away that you do not hear, and are drawn away, and worship other gods and serve them, I announce to you today that you shall surely perish; you shall not prolong your days in the land which you cross over the Jordan to go in and possess. I call heaven and earth as witnesses today against you, that I have set before you life and death, blessing and cursing; therefore, choose life, that both you and your descendants may live" (Deut. 30:15-19).

This is the choice God places before His people in every generation. It is the choice facing every Christian living in the United States of America today — life or death. The choice is up to you.

Since 1973 and the infamous *Roe v. Wade* decision, a

generation of Americans have been choosing death and cursing, rather than life and blessing.

There are many ways you can choose to support life. You could work as a counselor at a crisis pregnancy center, or open your home to an unwed mother who needs a place to stay until her child is born. Perhaps you could consider adopting an unwanted or special needs child. All of God's children deserve to have a mother and a father who will love them and raise them in the nurture and admonition of the Lord.

According to Dr. Land, "We need to put our money where our mouth is, open our doors, and be willing to minister to those in need."

The freedoms we enjoy today and the secondary blessings that have resulted from the preaching of the gospel in America can no longer be taken for granted.

Francis Schaeffer, in speaking to a group of Christians several years ago, said we have already let many of our freedoms slip through our fingers. "Not a hundred years ago," he said. "It's been in our lifetime, in the last 40 years that these things have happened."

What has slipped through our fingers? The freedom of our children and teachers to pray and read the Bible in the public schools. The freedom to protect by law the lives of unborn human babies. The freedom to publicly pray and protest at the sites where the killing takes place.

Patrick Buchanan, in *Right from the Beginning,* quotes Bernanos who wrote of another time, "To be a reactionary today may simply mean to be alive because only a corpse does not react anymore against the maggots teaming upon it."

In other words, "Wake up! Shake off the maggots!"

We must be willing to speak out against the evils in our land today. If we don't, who will?

12

At the Point of No Return?

It was given to us to learn at the outset
that life is a profound and passionate
thing. — Justice Holmes

Peter Marshall explains the meaning of the "point of no return:"

> On a trans-Atlantic airliner, as the naviga-
> tor plots the plane's projected coarse, at a
> certain point he will make a neat dot and
> circle it and label it PNR. Once that point
> is passed, for the plane to go back to its
> point of departure, would require more
> fuel than remains on board. The plane has
> just passed the Point of No Return (PNR).
> America has not yet reached that point.

Or has it?

Charles Colson, speaking at the 1994 dedication of the new facilities for Focus on the Family, stated, "America has five years."

The late Francis Schaeffer said, "This may be our last chance."

George Barna, who heads the Barna Research Group,

told the East Side Foursquare Church in Kirkland, Washington, "Beneath the surface of this facade we call civilization, there is seething racial, economic, and ethnic unrest in America."

Then he made this startling statement: "We have five to seven years before anarchy breaks out in this country — unless there is a moral and spiritual awakening." And he added, "I'm not hopeful."

Neither is United Press Syndicate columnist Richard Reeves. After the riot that followed the Rodney King beating and subsequent trial in Los Angeles that acquitted the four policemen involved, Reeves wrote on May 1992 that he had "seen the future, and it must be stopped."

Reeves describes the mood of south central L.A. as black men gathered to hear the judge's ruling on whether one of the policemen, Lawrence Powell, would be tried again on one of the brutality charges. As he stood on the street, wondering what would happen if Powell got off, Reeves knew the answer: "It means more trouble."

According to Reeves, the potential exists for a deadly race war in our nation:

> The Los Angeles police were criticized for retreating at the outbreak of the riot; I'm not sure they had a choice. Can a few thousand men though trained and disciplined stand up to tens of thousands or even hundreds of thousands of undisciplined men, who are just as well armed and a lot more ready to die? I doubt that the situation is much better in several other American cities. . . .
>
> Unless we do something about this very quickly, we will see the crossfire next time. Both sides are armed now, the people

who run Washington don't much care. And
the thin blue line of police, from what I
have seen here, may not know it. The army
will have to come in and perhaps stay.
Order will be restored, the rage and bitter-
ness will be driven underground.

Soon, in five years, perhaps in ten, I
can only guess, we will have organized
domestic terrorism in the United States.

Race riots and domestic terrorism may be only one
sign of impending danger.

Peter Marshall, writing in *The Light and the Glory*,
lists some of the social indicators that show God's hand of
mercy may be lifting off America: "the rapidly decaying
morality, the disintegrating American family, the acceptance of rebellion and violent crime as the norm for
modern life." Then, he adds a more recent modern phe-
nomenon that also seems to bare witness to our impending
judgment:

There have been earthquakes and droughts
and floods. There have been untimely frosts,
a slight but significant drop in the average
mean temperature, and freak weather conditions which have lately seen hurricanes
in California, more snow in northern Florida
than in Cape Cod, and the worst winter in
the East in our history. Add to this the new
strains of crop blight and infestation, which
technology seems no longer able to check,
and to borrow a phrase from the Puritans,
"It would seem that God's Controversy
with America has begun in earnest."

No one can deny that the hour is late, and the judgment of God may already have begun to fall.

A Fool's Paradise?

During a recent interview, Marshall, made these sobering comments:

> I think we are in the ninth inning. I think it's extremely late in this country. I think we are on the edge of real national self-destruction. I think that we are looking at the very strong probability of economic collapse unless there is a tremendous change. We are going to spend ourselves, tax ourselves into total oblivion. The national debt is totally out of control. I think it is ballistic now.

We are living in a fool's paradise. It's almost over for America unless we turn back to God.

But why should we be shocked? God makes it clear that when a nation passes laws and makes policies that run counter to His Word, that nation invokes His wrath and deserves His judgment. In a sense, that nation abrogates its authority.

> The instant I speak concerning a nation and concerning a kingdom to pluck up, to pull down and to destroy it, if that nation against whom I have spoken turns from its evil, I will relent of the disaster that I have thought to bring upon it (Jer. 18:7-8).

Unless there is a moral and spiritual awakening in this country, our children and grandchildren will not live in the same kind of country in which you and I grew up. I don't think any of us are aware of what's actually happening in America today, but the little I know troubles me deeply.

Why are we so prone to turn away from God? Why this antipathy toward the Creator?

Why is God considered the enemy? Why does man seek other gods to worship when the One True God has provided for us everything for this life and the one to come?

God asked the same question of Israel — the people He had raised, nourished, nurtured, and provided for:

> What injustice have your fathers found in Me, that they have gone far from Me, have followed idols, and have become idolaters? . . . I brought you into a bountiful country, to eat its bountiful fruit and its goodness. But when you entered, you defiled My land and made My heritage an abomination (Jer. 2:5,7).

Like fools, we have followed the idols of greed, pleasure, entertainment, and lust. We have defiled the New World paradise of our forefathers with the blood of millions of innocent babies. We have made our godly heritage an abomination by condoning and coddling those who pervert themselves with unnatural, inhuman acts of lust.

Like the Israelites, are we not inviting God's wrath?

> Therefore, I will yet bring charges against you," says the Lord, "and against your children I will bring charges. . . . My people have changed their Glory for what does not profit. Be astonished, O heavens, at this, and be horribly afraid; be very desolate," said the Lord. "For My people have committed two evils: They have forsaken Me, the fountain of living waters, and hewn

themselves cisterns — broken cisterns that can hold no water (Jer. 2:9,11-13).

The Measure of Guilt

Do you wonder what God thinks of America — the most God-blessed nation on earth, which for a hundred and fifty years has underwritten 91 percent of the world's missions' bills, but now exports its corruption to others?

Pastor Jess Moody made a frightening observation: "Guilt is measured by the amount of light rejected."

We have only to look back 60 years to find an example of a nation that rejected the light of the gospel and suffered terribly for her sin. Germany had been the hub of the Protestant Reformation that brought the Church out of the Dark Ages and into the light of God's Word. Martin Luther, John Calvin, John Huss, Wycliffe, Savonarola, and others led the way for Christianity to become the most powerful social force in history.

That force, however, was dealt a blow, when, as we have already discussed, the Age of Enlightenment warped men's minds with humanistic ideas. The resulting terror of the French Revolution spawned a spirit of violence that carried over into the twentieth century and found its embodiment in one man — Adolf Hitler.

Somewhere along the line, the German people abandoned their historical and religious roots.

What can we as Christian Americans do to keep from falling into the same trap? One very simple preventative is to rediscover the original vision that our forefathers had for America.

Richard C. Halverson, a former chaplain of the U.S. Senate, has said, "We have lost the spiritual moral anchor that secured our nation from its earliest critical days. We are at sea without compass, direction, or destination."

Someone else has said, "We are a rootless society

unaware of how we got here or the price paid for our freedom."

The rewriting of American history has resulted in a generation of young people who are ignorant of the glorious history of our country. But, that can be easily remedied, at least by anyone who has a desire to learn the truth.

As Christian parents and grandparents, we can study our nation's history from reliable sources and teach the facts to our children and grandchildren. Accurate and positive accounts of United States history can be found in the textbooks produced by reliable publishers and used in many Christian schools.

We must encourage children and adults alike to read the biographies of some of our nation's great leaders, like George Washington, Thomas Jefferson, Benjamin Franklin, Abraham Lincoln, and others.

If we don't learn the truth about America's past and strive to recover our Christian heritage, we may find ourselves unable to stand against the political pressures of the future.

When the Church Withdraws

The German Lutheran church, in the late 1930s, having already abandoned the message of the true gospel of Jesus Christ, passed a resolution condemning Jews. Author Erwin Lutzer quotes the Lutheran's spokesman, Herman Grunner, who made clear what they stood for:

> The time is fulfilled for the German people and Hitler. It is because of Hitler that Christ, God the Helper and Redeemer, has become effective among us. Therefore, national socialism is positive Christianity in action. Hitler is the way of the Spirit and

the will of God for the German people to
enter the church of Christ.

The church bearing the name of one of history's
greatest theologians, Martin Luther, had bowed its knee to
the pagan god of secular humanism at its worst. The
German church bought into the lie that "man is the
measure of all things" and he can solve his own problems.

Although Hitler used the German church to his own
advantage, he advocated the same philosophy that is
bandied about in America today — the separation of
church and state.

Billy Falling, author of *The Political Mission of the
Church,* provides insight into Hitler's "theology":

> Remember what Hitler did in the Third
> Reich? He said, "I will protect the German
> people, you take care of the church. You
> pastors should worry about getting people
> to heaven and leave this world to me."

Some church leaders stood up to the fuhrer, as we
discussed in an earlier chapter. Bishop Niemoller, like
many today, gave this challenge: "As Christians and men
of the church we, too, have a responsibility for the
German people, laid upon us by God. Neither you nor
anyone else can take that away from us."

Unfortunately, Niemoller was in the minority, and
"his fellow bishops collapsed into unconditional support
for Hitler, pledging to carry out any measures and direc-
tives he ordered." Falling records the tragic consequences
of the church's silence:

> Millions of God's chosen people went to
> the gas chamber because good men had left
> "this world" to the leadership to a godless
> man. Nor were they alone. Although 6

million Jews died, 13 million people of other nationalities died, many because they believed in God, helped His people, and resisted the evil that was embodied in Adolf Hitler.

Many believe that the tragedy of World War II was the direct result of one factor: the withdrawal of the Church from the political arena.

What will happen if we, as God's church, relegate ourselves to caring for the souls of people while expressing little concern for the civil authority in which we live? Will the Church in America be held responsible if our nation collapses morally, or bows its knee to a godless demagogue like Adolf Hitler? Will we bear "the measure of guilt" for having the light but not letting it shine in our society and our culture — and yes, in our politics?

The real issue is not between Church and state. The problem is that the Church has stood by like the bishops of Germany while the state took control of the religious establishment.

The civil government of America has claimed neutrality while establishing humanism as the religion of this country. No longer is Christianity the foundation of our society with the Bible the source of its morality. The humanists among us believe that the mind of man is the source of all true reason and morality.

What is the result? John Whitehead, in the preface of his book, *Religious Apartheid,* sums up humanism's effects on our society:

> Unborn children as sanctioned by the Supreme Court, are the targets of private interest groups as well as state agencies that not only want to abort them but harvest their body parts as well. The homosexual

movement has blossomed into a national gay agenda that is altering politics, education, the church, the arts, and the family.

What can we do to avoid repeating the mistakes of the past made by our brothers in pre-war Germany?

Get Involved!

Many Christians have abandoned the educational and political process and left important national decisions to others who are not acquainted with America's heritage.

John W. Whitehead notes that "what we are witnessing is the end of religion and morality in the public sphere. As Christianity is driven further from the marketplace, American public life is increasingly vulnerable to radical lifestyles."

Who shoulders the blame for these negative changes in the fabric of American culture? Government leaders? The Supreme Court? In part; but who else is to blame?

"Past generations of Christians and other religionists who were not involved in society or who sat silently by as the culture embraced the secular world view are also greatly responsible," says Whitehead.

Billy Falling, in his book, *The Political Mission of the Church*, notes that "the question is not just *can* we challenge the political process. We must settle in our minds the question of whether or not this is God's will for us."

To settle this question, Falling refers us to the thirteenth chapter of Romans: "Let every soul be subject to the governing authorities. For there is no authority except from God, and the authorities that exist are appointed by God" (Rom. 13:1).

Falling says this verse should give us an idea of the importance that God places on government. He then asks,

Are we so "spiritual" that we are not interested in civic bodies? Then we are more "spiritual" than God himself. Government is an integral part of the plan of God for men. We cannot place less value on it than God does.

America's greatness is the direct result of the Church's theology of civil government. "If there had been no Bible, there would have been no Constitution. If their had been no Christianity, there would not have been a United States of America," writes Falling.

Erwin W. Lutzer in his book, *Why Are We the Enemy?* writes the following:

The return of the church to the cultural debate is long overdue, but high profile activism involves risk, the possibility of being misunderstood, a backlash that paints us with the same brush as the fanatics.

What can we do to counteract the adversarial and threatening image of the Church that now pervades our culture? How can we who are perceived as enemies reach out to heal our wounded nation? We must not retreat from the fray because the battle has taken an ugly turn. Indeed, is retreat even possible? Is it possible to simply go back to our Bible studies, seeking to "live and let live" while attempting to present the gospel to society?

Jack Kemp asks, "How can we say we are Christians and not get involved in politics?"

It is a valid question.

Fulfilling Our Political Mission

ABC and *New York Times* exit polls of voters in 1984 found that of the 89 million people who voted, only 15 percent — 13.3 million — were born-again Christians. In recent years, however, the number of Christians going to the polls has increased, mainly because the Christian media — radio, television, and print — have made us more aware of the issues.

More recent surveys show that about 78 percent of evangelical Christians are registered to vote, but only 54 percent actually go to the polls on election day.

Why do the other 46 percent stay home? Apparently, they don't care who gets elected, and that's exactly why we're in the mess we're in today. Or maybe, as Stephen Strang of *Charisma* magazine suggests, "They think their focus should be on heavenly things, not on dirty, earthly things like politics."

According to Billy Falling, in America today, more than 136 million citizens are members of over 357 thousand Christian churches, with an annual cash flow in access of $48 billion. With those kinds of numbers and resources, we could elect any candidate of our choice.

What can we do to get people more involved in the political process of our nation? Billy Falling suggests we begin by educating church people to see the rightful place that God's church has in the political arena.

"This is no small task," he says. "After all, we have held back from participation for years. Changing misconception to truth and opening up the truth of teaching about the Christian in government is not going to be easy. Still, God is speaking to many people today, and together we can make a mighty impact."

To do this, Fallings says will require the participation of "every church and every pastor and church leader." He believes a "portion of the local church budget needs to be set aside for the fulfillment of this political mission."

Christians need "to stop sidestepping the political issue," says Falling, and "clearly proclaim the political mission of the Church. Only when we call it what it is will we be able to make headway on the solution."

Aside from voting and supporting conservative candidates, Billy Falling believes Christians should be producing winning candidates from among their own church members. There are only "95,180 elected officials in the nation today, including congressmen, state legislators, city councilmen, school board members, mayors, governors, and elected judges," says Falling. "If only one-third of the churches of America could produce a winning candidate for office, Christians would occupy every public office."

Into the Arena!

In the 1994 elections, Christians were more active than ever before in the political process, provoking a media firestorm. Christians were labeled everything from "intolerant hatemongers" to "radicals outside the mainstream of America." The negative reporting shouldn't startle us since only 8 percent of people in the news media attend church or synagogue regularly.

Former Texas Governor Ann Richards, while waging her losing battle against George Bush Jr., claimed that by permitting conservative Christians to take part in the state GOP convention, it had "invited a Trojan horse into its midst."

This "radical fringe," as described by one conservative delegate, is the business people, Boy Scout leaders, teachers, home owners, and taxpayers of the community! "How radical is that?" she asked in an interview with *Citizen* magazine.

Republican Representative Jack Kingston of Georgia, also quoted in *Citizen,* notes that "an overwhelming portion of the electorate shares the mainstream agenda of safe neighborhoods, limited government, strong families, and schools that work."

William Bennett, writing in *The Devaluing of America,* reached a similar conclusion:

> While contemporary liberalism has moved away from and, in some cases, even against the mainstream of American political life, today's conservatism is more at home with the common sense and the common beliefs of the American people. Conservatives should be encouraged about that; American's are an optimistic lot.

Part of the problem with the world's perception of the Church comes from the fact that we are not "of this world" and our "citizenship is in heaven." This creates tension, but "tension is relevant to a life of faith," as someone has said.

We should not be surprised that the world hates us. After all, Jesus said, "If the world hates you, you know that it hated Me before it hated you," (John 15:18).

Sometimes, however, I wonder if we haven't contributed to the negative way the world views Christians. Instead of exemplifying the life of Christ, too often Christians are arrogant and argumentative.

Scripture teaches, "And a servant of the Lord must not quarrel but be gentle to all" (2 Tim. 2:24).

William Bennett brilliantly makes this point in *The Devaluing of America.* Although he admits to being called "combative," Bennett says, "I don't mind. I've always tried to be very direct and candid. Americans like straight talk." Then he adds this qualifying virtue: "I always speak with good will — that is, with the hope of arriving at a conclusion that we can all share."

How can we promote good will? Bennett suggests we "improve our disposition" and "cheer up!"

After all, our hope is not in this life. We will have all of eternity to live in a perfect kingdom, governed by a loving King, with all our needs met.

Until then, however, we need to lovingly, gently work to make the society in which God has placed us the best it can be for all our citizens. And to do that, we need to elect godly men and women who consider government service as part of their Christian calling.

The Power of One!

As long as God's people are alive and well, there is hope for America.

Christian people ought to permeate and penetrate every aspect of our society: education, government, the media. It is a tragedy that for too long the people of God have abandoned law, journalism, and the entertainment industry. Our involvement is long overdue.

What can you do?

First of all, *do something!* Remember, when good men do nothing, evil triumphs.

Columnist Ann Melvin suggests that we turn our outrage into action:

> Do something. Become informed, participate in the electoral process, let your voice be heard, write your president, senator, preacher, principal, mayor, city councilman.
>
> One person? No! One and one and one and one and one, and the ones add up. . . .
>
> And don't start whining. What good

does it do to complain? The day we quit standing for what is good and right just because it doesn't get immediate results is the day the end begins. We stand for what is right and against what is wrong simply because we must.

The power of one is the whole idea upon which the freedom of man is found, and so get a grip.

Why?

Why not?

The second thing you can do is *stand for something*.

Gary Bauer, in his message "What Happened in America?" suggests some things that deserve our attention and allegiance:

For millions of Americans . . . life is not about judicial decisions and executive decrees. It's helping hands and good neighbors. It's nighttime prayers and lovingly packed lunch boxes. It's hard work and a little money put away for the future.

No government commands those things; no government replicates them. They are done naturally, out of love and a commitment to the future.

Stand for those things, believe in those things, teach your children those things, live for those things, vote for candidates who understand those things.

If you will do that, I am absolutely convinced that this great experiment in liberty under God, this shining city upon a hill, will survive for your children and for mine.

Helen Kromer, in the musical review *For Heaven Sake*, has caught the thrust of this thought in her chorus: "One Man Awake."

> One man awake can waken another.
> The second can waken his next door brother.
> The three awake can rouse a town,
> By turning the whole place upside-down.
> The many awake can make such a fuss.
> That it finally awakens the rest of us.
> One man up with dawn in his eyes, multiplies.

One such man with "dawn in his eyes" was George Washington. He had the vision for America in his heart and refused to let it die.

In *The Light and the Glory*, Peter Marshall tells the story of how this great leader took time from his private life to start a letter writing campaign to the most influential men in America at the time. Pleading that "something must be done" to save the union or "the fabric will fall, for it is certainly tattering."

As a result of Washington's persistence, the Constitutional Convention was convened in Philadelphia in May 1787, resulting in the writing of one of the greatest documents in history — the United States Constitution. And it all began — with one letter.

Every Christian who loves this nation and longs to see her restored to her original heritage must get involved. If we do not, we may find ourselves, like the prewar church in Germany, carrying the full measure of guilt for having abandoned the political arena — and leaving it, like an orphan, in the hands of a cruel taskmaster.

13

A Rising or a Setting Sun

My kingdom is not of this world.
— Jesus

Much of our focus in this book has been on America's government and politics, where we've gone wrong and what we need to do to change the direction our nation is headed.

At this point, however, we need to remember that the early church changed their world, turning it upside down, without any of the advantages of political clout, satellite communication, air travel, or computer technology — and, within a governmental system that was totally hostile to the Christian Church.

Pastor Jack Hayford noted, "The early church changed world history not by militant activism or the power of the vote, but by the power of love and a fidelity in the way they lived."

Why were the first Christians so successful? Because their focus was primarily eternal — and ours must be as well. Man's eternal welfare is far more important than conditions in the here and now.

Richard Halverson writes, "It is clear in Scripture that the will of God is preeminently for the *eternal* welfare of mankind not simply his earthly condition here and now."

Columnist Cal Thomas recalled a conversation he had with Billy Graham shortly after he returned from his 1982 trip to the Soviet Union. Some religious leaders had denounced the visit, saying that Graham was putting his seal of approval on Communism.

Thomas asked Graham if he felt that he was being used.

"Of course," the great preacher answered, "but I'm using them, too — to get out the gospel."

As a result, Graham was able to speak privately to the nation's highest leaders, telling them they had nothing to fear from loosening their grip on the Church. "Years later," Thomas notes, "the opening of Russia to religious freedom vindicated him."

It is more important to save a soul than it is to win an election. We must not get sidetracked and let people go to hell while we are parading and protesting with placards and petitions.

Richard Halverson puts it this way:

> Anger over an ever-increasing bureaucracy with its exorbitant taxes, its growing centralized control, its mounting deficit, its dehumanizing legislation, its immorality, its indifference to spiritual and eternal realities is understandable. But such emotion ought not to replace an evangelical compassion and concern for the eternal lostness of mankind.

No amount of political action will save our nation if the Lord turns His face away from us. "Unless the Lord builds the house, they labor in vain who build it. Unless the Lord guards the city, the watchman stays awake in vain" (Ps. 127:1).

Columnist Cal Thomas wrote that "political power alone is not going to usher in the moral and spiritual revival that . . . Americans seek and the nation needs."

Francis Schaeffer warned us 20 years ago about "conservative humanism" — you can believe right about economic theory and foreign policy and still go to hell.

We need to get our priorities straight, without being judgmental.

The late J. Vernon Magee, the radio biblical expositor, once said, "I have preached few messages on hell."

That may sound strange coming from a person who believed the Bible to be the inerrant Word of God. But he explained: "I'm not given to tears, and I've always believed that, when you talk about hell, you should say it with tears."

We must remember that, as the Church — the body of Christ — we are a heavenly people, and our mission field is a pagan society. As Christians, we must assume responsibility for our nation.

In chapter nine of the Book of Daniel, the prophet and statesman confesses before God the sins of his nation. Although he, no doubt, had not committed these sins himself, he identified himself with his people and stood in the gap for them.

And so must we. In crying out against the sins of our nation, we must be reminded that Jesus Christ came into the world to save sinners.

We must not assume the role of self-appointed protectors of the nation's morality. The snide remark and strident voice must yield to reason and reasoning. We need not abandon our convictions to engage in dialogue with those holding different views. We must remember that "the weapons of our warfare are not carnal but mighty in God for pulling down strongholds" (2 Cor. 10:4).

Peter Marshall puts it this way:

If we Christians think that simply by political involvement we are going to turn the country around, we're crazy. If we think that we can adopt an antagonistic triumphalism that says we are going to get organized and throw all the bad guys out and take over, we will be brought face to face with our own sinfulness.

This does not discount the impact that the Church and virtuous people should have in the life and times of our nation. It is not to take away from the need for political action; it is to underscore the fact that Jesus Christ remains as always the central theme in history.

Richard Halverson writes, "Christians *ought* to be involved in translating faith into life in this world. The danger is that secondary issues are given priority to the neglect of essentials." He goes on to say we must not abandon our "unique solutions for human changes."

In this last chapter I want to discuss these "unique solutions" — what only you and I, as God's people, can do to bring America back to her moral and spiritual roots. Every American can vote and get involved in the political arena, but as the church of Jesus Christ, we can do more. Not only *can* we do more; there are some things *only* you and I can do!

The Final Formula

What should we do to prevent America's collapse? We must take the three steps, outlined in 2 Chronicles 7:14, that lead to healing and restoration.

King Solomon had just completed the building of the temple, and the day of dedication seemed to be the dawning of a new era for the nation of Israel. Aware that His people were prone to turning away from His commands, God provided a formula for restoration should they find themselves under judgment:

> If My people who are called by My name will humble themselves, and pray and seek My face, and turn from their wicked ways, then I will hear from heaven, and will forgive their sin and heal their land (2 Chron. 7:14).

Let's look at what we as Christians must do:

1. Humble ourselves.
2. Pray and seek God.
3. Turn from our wicked ways.

Intertwined in many ways, these three prescriptions for our nation's ills work together to bring about the cure — forgiveness for us as a people and the healing of our land.

Notice, however, where the responsibility lies: "If my people." The responsibility for restoring the blessing of God upon our country rests with the people of God.

"If my people." If this country is destroyed, if it goes down in judgment, we won't be able to blame the politician, pornographer, abortion doctor, or the liquor merchant. The responsibility is mine — yours and mine.

God does not require the whole nation to repent, it is enough if only the Christians admit their sin and "turn from their wicked ways."

Peter Marshall writes:

> When William Stoddard once challenged Increase Mather on this very point as to whose responsibility it is, pointing out that the covenanted Christians in seventeenth century New England were only a fraction

of the population, Mather retorted that nonetheless that fraction was sufficient to "stand for the entire land" and "redeem the whole."

And so it is today. American Christians can "stand for the entire land" and "redeem the whole."

"If my people." What an awesome responsibility, but what a wonderful reason for hopefulness! That the people of God, though they may be few in number, even a remnant can petition the King of the universe and save an entire nation from destruction.

Humbling Ourselves

The first step to revival calls for God's people to "humble themselves." That means we have to do it as a free act of our will.

Dean Merrill's article, "Whatever Happened to Kneeling?" in *Christianity Today* cites this moving example of the need for American Christians to return to an old-fashioned form of humility:

> "The scene is the main ballroom of the Washington Hilton, January 1991, where two thousand politicians, captains of industry and other notables have gathered for the annual Leadership Luncheon. . . . On the dais waits the main speaker, television luminary and Atlanta pastor, Charles Stanley. His text is the familiar James 5:16, "The prayer of a righteous man is powerful and effective."
>
> He preaches eloquently and fervently about the need for America to humble itself before God as Elisha did and as Solomon and others did. But near the end of his

message he creeps out on a limb. Without raising his voice, he muses, "What would happen today if 2,000 people got on their knees, humbled themselves before God, and cried out for forgiveness?"

He drops a few more hints, and gradually the crowd realizes he's serious. He is talking about *them* getting on their knees — in their Brooks Brother suits. He allows that some may not be physically able, but for the rest he says, "Unless God does something in this nation, we are going to be humiliated in some fashion at some time. . . . I want to ask you if you will join me on my knees . . and pray until whenever the moderator thinks the time is over." With that he turns and drops from sight. End of sermon.

The ballroom goes quiet. There's a gradual shuffle of chairs and before long most of the crowd has followed his lead. A sober reverent mood fills the room. What Charles Stanley had the nerve to ask that day pertains to an ancient practice, gradually fading from contemporary Christianity.

What makes kneeling so different from sitting or standing before God? Merrill explains:

Kneeling reminds us who's in the dialogue. Prayer is not a couple of fellows chatting about the Dallas Cowboys. It is a human being coming face to face with his or her Supreme Authority, the ineffable God who is approachable, but still

278 • Come Home America

the One in charge. Thus, kneeling is a way of saying "I fully understand who's boss here, far be it from me to try to manipulate you or play games with you. I'm well aware of my status in this relationship, and I deeply appreciate you taking time to interact with me."

That is true humility. Bowing our hearts, our heads, and our knees before the Lord and acknowledging His awesome power and amazing grace.

"James, the Lord's brother and godly leader of the Jerusalem Church until A.D. 61 — when he was stoned to death," was a kneeler, notes Merrill. How do we know?

Merrill quotes the ancient writer Eusebius, who said of James, "He was in the habit of entering alone into the temple and was frequently found upon his knees begging forgiveness for the people so that his knees became hard like those of a camel, in consequence of his constantly bending them, in his work-worship of God."

Should this not be the main job of the Church — to beg forgiveness for our nation and our church? Only those who are truly humble will give themselves to such a low-profile, unassuming, difficult task.

Peter Marshall writes that "unless we Christians operate from a base of humility and lowliness . . . we will simply alienate people in our culture, instead of winning them because all that will come across is our antagonistic self-righteousness."

Why Should We Pray?

If this country goes to hell, we can't blame the politicians, the media, the pornographers, or Hollywood. No, it will be the fault of the people of God who didn't care — because God puts the responsibility to pray on us: "If

My people who are called by My name will humble themselves, and pray and seek My face. . . ."

Why should we pray? Some may wonder if America warrants God's judgment.

God did not spare Israel and Judah, and their sins were similar to America's today. The prophet Isaiah describes, in his warning to Israel, the conditions in their nation that were causing God to turn His face away from them:

> They say that what is right is wrong, and what is wrong is right; that black is white and white is black; bitter is sweet and sweet is bitter. Woe to those who are wise and shrewd in their own eyes! . . . Woe to those who are "heroes" when it comes to drinking, and boast about the liquor they can hold. They take bribes to pervert justice, letting the wicked go free and putting innocent men in jail (Isa. 5:20-23;TLB).

These verses read like the front page of today's newspaper.

Read this next indictment written by Isaiah, and consider it in light of our nation's sins of abortion, pride, and greed:

> For your hands are those of murderers and your fingers are filthy with sin. You lie and grumble and oppose the good. No one cares about being fair and true. Your lawsuits are based on lies; you spend your time plotting evil deeds and doing them. . . . You cheat and shortchange everyone. Everything you do is filled with sin; violence is your trademark (Isa. 59:3-6;TLB).

Has violence become America's trademark? What nation produces and exports more violent films? None. Many Third World countries — like China and India — will not even allow violent and R-rated movies to be shown.

What about America's cities, where injustice is turned back and ". . . truth has fallen in the streets" (Isa. 59:14).

Consider the fate of a nation that despises the Word of God, perverts justice, and whose "sins keep piling up before the righteous God" (Isa. 59:12). Isaiah tells us:

> Therefore, God will deal with them and burn them. They will disappear like straw on fire. Their roots will rot and their flowers wither, for they have thrown away the laws of God and despised the Word of the Holy One of Israel. That is why the anger of the Lord is against his people; that is why he has reached out his hand to smash them (Isa. 5:20-25;TLB).

God takes no pleasure in the destruction of a nation or the death of the wicked — or the righteous, for that matter. God loves you and your family. God loves America and wants to spare us from His judgment. But He cannot do it unless repentance prevails.

On the other hand, God says, sometimes it only takes one person to turn things around.

> "So I sought for a man among them who would make a wall, and stand in the gap before Me on behalf of the land, that I should not destroy it; but I found no one" (Ezek. 22:30).

God says: "I looked for some person to stand in the gap, and I couldn't find one." In fact, the Lord was amazed that there was no one who cared enough to stop the violence and injustice:

> Then the Lord saw it, and it displeased Him
> that there was no justice. He saw that there
> was no man, and wondered that there was
> no intercessor (Isa. 59:16).

God couldn't understand why no one was willing to intercede for the nation.

How many intercessors do you know? How many in your church meet faithfully to pray and petition God for our nation? How often do you set aside time for the sole purpose of touching the heart of God with your cries for mercy?

Have we ceased to be a praying people?

Peter Marshall, in his book, *The Light and the Glory*, writes that "two years after Washington assumed the presidency, a Southern Methodist preacher named Francis Aspinwall made a pilgrimage to New England, where the ground work of God's new Israel had first been laid."

What did Rev. Aspinwall find? After riding all over the countryside, through villages and towns, and visiting with the people, he came to this conclusion:

> I do feel as if there had been religion in this
> country once, and I apprehend there a little
> form and theory left. There may have been
> a praying people and ministry there, but I
> fear they are now dead.

Are there any praying people left in America or did they all die with the Pilgrims? I don't think so. In fact, there is a growing prayer movement in the United States that is making a difference.

We need prayer meetings, prayer in our homes, prayer in our churches. Christians must intercede on behalf of our nation, asking that God will turn us back to Him. If you know how to pray, you need to get hold of God — because our nation is in peril.

How Should We Pray?

Billy Falling, writing in *The Political Mission Of the Church,* notes that "Fulfilling our responsibility as citizens does not depend on how well our officials are doing their jobs. They must answer to God, and *we* must answer to God." That means we must pray earnestly before we cast our ballots on election day.

Once government officials are in office, we should continue to pray. The apostle Paul told Timothy, "Pray much for others; plead for God's mercy upon them; give thanks for all he is going to do for them. Pray in this way for kings and all others who are in authority over us, or are in places of higher responsibility" (1 Tim. 2:2;TLB).

Falling writes:

> If we are not asked by God to carry the responsibility of elected office, then we are charged with giving prayer support to those who do. This is no small thing, yet we often lightly add to our long list of prayer requests a few words for our leaders spiritual and political. Paul's strong words convey a lot more than a casual mention in a midweek prayer service.

Why should we pray for our leaders and government officials? So that "we may lead a quiet and peaceable life."

Falling says this means we should ask God to give us "a peaceful environment in which to live" and "the freedom to carry on godly lives, and to witness to those around us about His goodness."

We should also pray that they will be saved. Many of those who serve in government positions "are people of high ideals and good morals," writes Falling, "but their depth of conviction and dedication can be deepened by knowing Christ Jesus as Saviour. Let us pray that they will be saved."

In addition, those political leaders who *are* trying to live godly lives and serve Jesus Christ need our prayer support in even greater ways. They face great opposition from all sides. We need to pray that they, themselves, will be able, in the midst of political debate, to pray with holy hands lifted up to God, free from sin and anger and resentment" (2 Tim. 2:8;TLB).

What about government leaders who, through their words and deeds, are obviously not concerned about pleasing the Lord?

I read a most insightful article by Joseph L. Garlington, titled *Intercessors or Judges?* in which he told how the Lord dealt with him, about his judgment of certain politicians:

> We are called to intercede for our cities, governments, and leaders; but we are not to pray only for those who share our views. We must cry out to God on behalf of *all* people.
>
> The Church must grieve over the sins of our nation. We must agonize over the immorality that surrounds us and weep over the loss of innocent life. But we cannot afford to forget that our father Abraham stood before God Almighty and interceded on behalf of wicked Sodom. If we harbor a judgmental attitude toward our government, it will paralyze our ability to pray

with genuine faith.

The increasingly hostile and unchristian attitudes of many fellow Christians toward the Clinton administration has the potential to disqualify us as ambassadors of reconciliation.

As we approach the waning hours of this century, we have one obligation. We must stand in the gap and plead for mercy even if we don't think people deserve it. Jesus, not the church, is the judge of all humanity. We must make a choice: Will we be intercessors or judges?

Cal Thomas, in a column written in early 1993, noted that a group of 40 pro-life leaders wrote to evangelist Billy Graham requesting that he withdraw from offering the invocation and benediction at President Clinton's inauguration. Why? Because, they wrote, "the last thing we need is for a prominent and respected Christian leader to appear publicly with Clinton, to seemingly endorse his agenda."

Sound familiar? Thomas writes, "This was the same thing directed at Jesus Christ by religious leaders of his day. They were called Pharisees then, and they where scandalized that Jesus was hanging around too many prostitutes, tax collectors, and other people of low repute."

Cal Thomas then offers this stinging rebuke:

Those who would use the church as a platform from which to denounce the new president and who refuse to or only reluctantly pray for him are not only violating the Scripture in which they say that they believe, but are also closing off their access to the president-elect and any hope that they might have of changing Clinton's mind.

Any president's public policy should be critiqued, but he should have no doubt that even the critics of those policies hope that he does the right thing; according to the standard . . . in which he claims to believe. The chances of his doing the right thing are improved when he knows that people are praying for him.

The Sin Guarantee

Tim LaHaye notes that "America once legislated against those things that God says are wrong."

What happened to us? LaHaye explains:

> Gradually we began to tolerate, then accept, then condone openly, and even promote that which was once unthinkable. The perversion and degradation that once made us blush are now flaunted before the eyes of a nation that was conceived in the fear of God. It has happened little by little right before our eyes, not because someone forced it on us but seemingly because we did not care; we just didn't care.

In the first chapter of Romans, one point is plain and indisputable: "Sin leads to individual and collective ruin," writes Richard Halverson. "Sin guarantees the breakdown of all human social systems." There's only one solution to this breakdown: "righteousness exalts a nation" (Prov. 14:34).

What is "righteousness" — a word foreign to most of American society? Halverson notes that the word "righteousness" in both Hebrew and Greek is a simple word that clearly means "justice, virtue; it means to be chaste":

> It means to be right with God and right with
> your neighbor. It means purity in motive as
> well as propriety in method. It means rev-
> erence for God and concern for others. It
> means square-play, truthfulness, unself-
> ishness, humility, kindness, charity. It
> means Christ-likeness.

That means living your life as Jesus would.

Francis Schaeffer said, "This is true spirituality: Christ is Lord of *all* your life not just your religious life."

In recent studies, researcher George Barna pointed out that people are spending less time participating in church related activities. "Little more than one-third of Americans who describe themselves as Christians have read a Christian book other than the Bible in the last month," he writes.

What *have* they been reading? Or, maybe the question should be, what have they been *watching?*

Barna goes on to report that "some 80 percent of Christian young people, ages 18 to 26, viewed at least one movie in the theater in the last month." In fact, he says, "Christian young adults are more likely to watch MTV than non-Christian young adults."

Colorful Baptist preacher Jess Moody sums up America's entertainment problem: "We've invented tele-vision and don't have anything worth televising. We've invented computers to do our thinking, to be an enlarge-ment of our brain, when we don't use 5 percent of the brains we've got."

Summarizing his findings in the *1992-93 Barna Report,* published by Regal, Barna wrote, "Few areas of lifestyle apart from religious involvement made Chris-tians discernible from non-Christians."

Stephen Strang of *Charisma* magazine agrees, noting, "Given the way current entertainment trends are going, there's not much difference between how believers and non-believers have fun."

Strang then reaches this conclusion:

> Heaven help us. This generation of Americans has more leisure time than their grandparents ever dreamed of. Even people who work long hours spend 10 to 20 hours a week in a leisure activity, watching TV, reading a book, attending a sporting event, or going to a movie. At the same time, the Church is becoming more and more influenced by the spirit of this world. As our societies become more secularized, Christians have allowed a distinction between what they do on Sundays and what they do during the week.

To make matters worse, many churches seem to be watering down their message to appeal to the more secularized manner in which modern Christians live today.

Jess Moody puts it like this: "I'm tired of hearing that we must get away from our humble beginnings and shake the hayseed out of our hair and come of age. Of hearing about grandstand seats in glory but nothing about being a part of the sufferings of Jesus Christ."

Moody then asks, "When last did you hear a sermon on the suffering church?" This is his answer:

> Because the Church has danced to the political tunes of America and reflected its culture for so long, the Church has become just like the world, and there is no differ-

ence. So why should the Church suffer when it can get elected to any office it wants? We are hearing a lot about medals these days, but not much about scars.

Is the Church getting too sophisticated for a gospel that demands we "deny" ourselves "take up" our cross daily and follow Jesus? That commands we "lose" our lives for Jesus' sake? (See Luke 9:23-27.)

Jess Moody says he's "tired of trying to force a counterfeit kingdom of God upon an unregenerate society" and of hearing about how sophisticated we are when "we are the most gullible nation of all time."

How gullible are Americans? Demanding "freedom," our nation "throws the Ten Commandments out the window, and doesn't know the difference between love and lust," says Moody.

Many Christians, however, are afraid to challenge their fellow Americans with the truth. Instead, notes Moody, they "walk around the land nibbling their fingers afraid they are going to hurt someone's feelings when we have a nation that needs salt and light revealed unto them."

What does Moody suggest we do? "So stand up! Speak up! Believe up!"

Unless we as Christians get our act together and stop trying to be like the world, we will never impact our nation for good. God is calling us to personal discipline, to godly living, to a lifestyle that sets us apart from our pagan culture.

Dr. A.W. Tozer came to this conclusion: "God will wean us away from the world, the easy way if possible, the hard way if necessary."

Who Needs to Repent?

We as Christians are the people who need to repent: "If My people who are called by My name will . . . turn from their wicked ways. . . ."

This is the third and last of the three prescriptions in God's formula for healing our land. It may be last because repentance is the true test of whether we are really sincere about getting right with God. Repentance means making a complete about-face and turning away from our sin.

That is why God makes some wonderful promises concerning repentance:

> "The instant I speak concerning a nation and concerning a kingdom, to pluck up, to pull down and to destroy it, if that nation against whom I have spoken turns from its evil, I will relent of the disaster that I have thought to bring upon it" (Jer. 18:7-8).

On the other hand, God has some pretty harsh words for those who will not repent.

> "And the instant I speak concerning a nation and concerning a kingdom, to build and to plant it, if it does evil in my sight so that it does not obey My voice, then I will relent concerning the good with which I said I would benefit it" (Jer. 18:9-10).

In his book, *Right from the Beginning*, Patrick J. Buchanan writes about the results of America's moral decline:

> Now the descent from and disbelief in traditional Hebrew and Christian values and prescriptions is widespread. The routine deference once accorded the tradi-

tional churches is no longer proffered. In books and plays and films, priests and pastors and rabbis are mocked for the amusement of modernity.

We are a nation in conflict. And the conflict is over values. John Whitehead writes that "if the Judeo-Christian principles that served as the source of all law governing this Republic are not recovered in the near future, the conflict that will naturally emerge over the changes sweeping across the cultural landscape like a firestorm will destroy the structure of our country and its major institutions."

Whitehead then reaches this sobering conclusion:

As a cultural collapse due to opposing world views becomes more imminent, those supporting the system of religious apartheid in America will intensify the pressure, and oppression and even persecution of those who hold a religious world view may result.

Is that what we, as Christians, can expect? Oppression and persecution?

Peter Marshall warns that "if God continues to lift His grace as He has begun to, it will not be long before we will be in a hell very much of our own making."

We will have no one to blame but ourselves.

Marshall pulls no punches when he says, "I think we've used up the spiritual capital. I think we have about bled the bank account dry. I think we are out of time. We're looking at one of two things. Either there's going to be a national revival, or it's total destruction."

How can we bring about revival? With "ongoing repentance," says Marshall. "By that I mean facing up to our own sinfulness and our own shortcomings."

The church must acknowledge its part in the moral decline of our nation and ask God to forgive us for not preventing the tidal wave of unbelief that now waits poised to engulf this great land.

Six times in its history our nation has turned back to God. I believe it could happen again. Today, there are hopeful signs. But the time to act is now.

The handwriting on the wall need not be a death sentence to hope but an encouragement to faith — an invitation to "Come home America!"

Resource List

Books

Abortion — Toward an Evangelical Consensus. Paul B. Fowler. Portland, OR: Multnomah, 1987.

Absolute Confusion. George Barna. Ventura, CA: Regal Books, 1993.

The Adams Family. James Truslow Adams. New York, NY: Blue Ribbon Books, 1930.

America: To Pray or Not to Pray. David Barton. Aledo, TX: David Barton, 1988.

American Historical Documents. Harvard Classics. Danbury, CT: Grolier Enterprises Corp., 1980.

American History Before 1877. Ray A. Billington. Totowa, NJ: Littlefield, Adams, & Co., 1965.

The American Mind. Henry Steele Commager. New Haven & London: Yale University Press, 1950.

A Basic History of the U.S. Clarence B. Carson. Wadley, AL: American Textbook Committee, 1994.

The Best of Peter Marshall. Catherine Marshall. New York, NY: Guideposts, 1983.

Builders of the Bay Colony. Samuel Eliot Morison. Boston, MA: Northeastern University, 1930.

Bulwark of the Republic. Benton J. Hendrick. Boston, MA: Little, Brown & Co., 1937.

The Christian History of the Constitution of the United States of America. Joseph Allan Montgomery. San Francisco, CA: Foundation for American Christian Education, 1966.

A Christian Manifesto. Francis Schaeffer. Wheaton, IL: Crossway Books, 1981.

Classics of Protestantism. Vergilius Ferm, Editor. New York, NY: Philosophical Library, 1959.

The Closing of the American Mind. Allan Bloom. New York, NY: Simon & Schuster, 1989.

The Creation of the American Republic, 1776-1787. Gordon S. Wood. Chapel Hill, NC: The University of North Carolina Press, 1969.

Cry of the Innocents. John O. Anderson. South Plainfield, NJ: Bridge Publishing, 1984.

The Culture of Disbelief. Stephen Carter. New York, NY: BasicBooks, 1993.

A Dance With Death. Charles Colson. Dallas, TX: Word Publishers, 1993.

The Day America Told the Truth. James Patterson and Peter Kimm. New York, NY: Prentice Hall Press, 1991.

Democracy in America. Alexis de Tocqueville. New York, NY: Mentor Books, 1956.

The Devaluing of America. William J. Bennett. New York, NY: Simon & Schuster, 1992.

Faith of Our Founding Fathers. Tim LaHaye. Brentwood, TN: Wolgemuth & Hyatt, 1987.

The Fall of the Ivory Tower. George Roche, Washington, DC: Regnery Publishers, 1994.

The Five Thousand Year Leap. W. Cleon Skousen. Washington, DC: National Center for Constitutional Studies, 1981.

A History of Colonial America. Max Sanelle & Robert Middekauff. New York, NY: Holt, Rinehart, & Winston, 1964.

Honest John Adams. Gilbert Chinard. Boston, MA: Little, Brown Co., 1933.

The Index of Leading Cultural Indicators. William J. Bennett. New York, NY: Simon & Schuster, 1994.

Inventing America. Garry Wills, Garden City, NY: Doubleday, 1978.

Jefferson. Albert Jay Nack. Rahway, NJ: Harcourt, Brace, & Co., 1926.

Jonathan Edwards, The Preacher. Ralph Turnbull. Grand Rapids, MI: Baker Book House, 1958.

The Light and The Glory. David Manuel and Peter Marshall. Tarrytown, NY: Fleming H. Revell, 1977.

Lives and Graves of Our Presidents. G.S. Weaver. Chicago, IL: Elder Publishing Co., 1884.

The Living U.S. Constitution. Saul K. Padover. New York, NY: New American Library, 1983.

Miracle at Philadelphia. Catherine Drinker Bowen. Boston, MA: Little, Brown, & Co., 1966.

A Nation at Risk. The National Commission of Excellence in Education, 1983.

The National Review College Guide: America's 50 Top Liberal Arts Schools. Charles Sykes and Brad Miner, Editors. Brentwood, TN: Wolgemuth & Hyatt, 1991.

New Basic History of the U.S. Charles A. & Mary R. Beard, Garden City, NY: Doubleday, 1944.

The Political Mission of the Church. Billy Falling. Valley Center, CA: Billy Falling Publishing, 1990.

The Rebirth of America. Nancy Leigh DeMoss, Editor. Philadelphia, PA: The Arthur S. DeMoss Foundation, 1986.

Religion in American Public Life. A. James Reichley. Washington, DC: The Brookings Institution, 1985.

Religious Apartheid. John W. Whitehead. Chicago, IL: Moody Press, 1994.

The Return of the Puritans. Patricia O. Brooks. Springdale, PA: Whitaker House, 1976.

The Rewriting of America's History. Catherine Millard. Camp Hill, PA: Horizon House, 1991.

Right From the Beginning. Patrick J. Buchanan. Washington, DC, Regnery Gateway, 1990.

The Rise and Fall of the Third Reich. William L. Shirer. New York, NY: Simon & Schuster, 1960.

The Rockets Red Glare. Richard J. Barnet. New York, NY: Simon & Schuster, 1990.

The Roots of American Order. Russell Kirk. Washington, DC: Regnery Gateway, 1991.

School Choice. David Harmer. Washington, DC: Cato Institute, 1994.

The 7 Habits of Highly Successful People. Stephen R. Covey. New York, NY: Simon & Schuster, 1989.

The Sexual Dead-End. Stephen Green. London: Broadview Books, 1992.

Sodom's Second Coming. F. LaGard Smith. Eugene, OR: Harvest House, 1993.

They Gathered At the River. Bernard A. Weisberger. Chicago, IL: Quadrangle Paperbacks, 1966.

This Freedom, Whence? J. Wesley Bready. New York, NY: American Tract Society, 1946.

The Timelessness of Jesus Christ: His Relevance in Today's World. Richard Halverson. Ventura, CA: Regal Books, 1982.

To Pray or Not to Pray. Charles Wesley Lowry. Washington, DC: University Press, 1963.

Under God: Religion and American Politics. Garry Wills. New York, NY: Simon & Schuster, 1990.

What Are They Teaching Our Children? Mel and Norma Gabler. Wheaton, IL: Victor Books, 1985.

Whatever Became of Sin? Carl Menninger. Toronto/New York, NY: Bantam Books, 1978.

When the Wicked Seized the City. Chuck and Donna McIlheny. Lafayette, IN: Huntington House, 1993.

Why America Doesn't Work. Charles Colson. Dallas, TX: Word Publishing, 1991.

Why Are We the Enemy? Erwin W. Lutzer. Chicago, IL: Moody Press, 1993.

Tapes

"Sanctity of Life — Taking a Stand." Dr. Richard Land. Southern Baptist Convention, Nashville, TN.

"A Christian Manifesto." Dr. Francis Schaeffer. Coral Ridge Ministries, P.O. Box 40, Fort Lauderdale, FL 33302.

"Education in America: The Biblical Basis." Rev. Peter Marshall. Tape of the Month, 36 Nickerson Road, Orleans, MA 01653.

Speaking Engagements

Dan Johnson is available for
speaking engagements for
churches, conferences, and schools.

Please contact:

DAN JOHNSON
P.O. Box 42460
Tacoma, WA 98442, USA